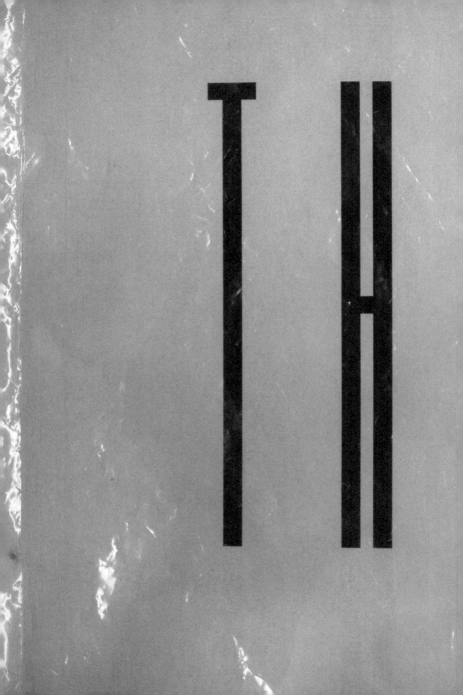

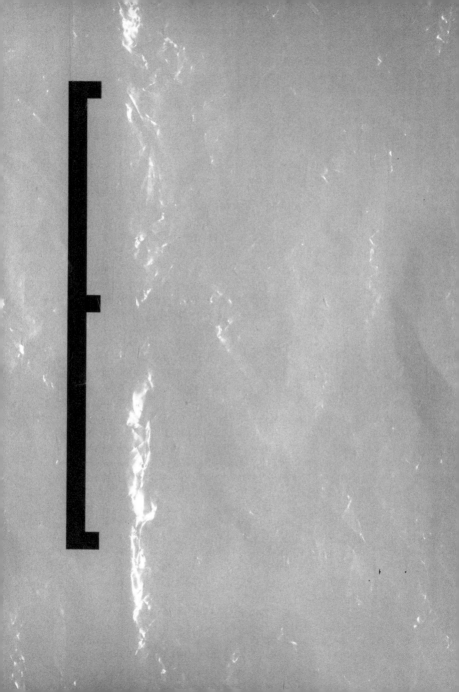

WAVE BOOKS

SEATTLE/NEW YORK

Published by Wave Books

www.wavepoetry.com

Wave Books titles are distributed to the trade by

Consortium Book Sales and Distribution

Phone: 800-283-3572 / SAN 631-760X

Library of Congress Cataloging-in-Publication Data

Names: Rohrer, Matthew, author.

Title: The others / Matthew Rohrer.

Description: First edition. | Seattle : Wave Books, [2017]

Identifiers: LCCN 2016030568| ISBN 9781940696416

(limited edition hardcover) | ISBN 9781940696409 (softcover)

Classification: LCC PS3568.O524 A6 2017 | DCC 811/.54—dc23

LC record available at https://lccn.loc.gov/2016030568

Designed and composed by Quemadura

Printed in the United States of America

9 8 7 6 5 4 3 2 1

First Edition

Wave Books 063

escending the subway stairs
in a crowd of others, slow
steps, everyone a little
hunched in their coats, probably
as unhappy as I was
to have to go to work.
At least I always assumed
the others hated their jobs
too. *That's why they call it work*
my wife always says, but she
was raised in austerity;
the idea of hating
a job seemed a luxury
to her. I didn't know. My knee
hurt for some reason, my hip
felt a little out of joint.
I couldn't imagine why,
maybe psychosomatic.

I was still on the staircase;
someone in front of me stopped
to get on their phone the last
beams of coverage, holding
up everyone on their slow
reluctant ways down
to the subway platform
to be carried noisily
to work. I felt like I knew
these people though we never
spoke, we just glanced furtively
at each other every day
or together rolled our eyes
when an old Caribbean woman
stood up and started
at the top of her high-pitched
patois to preach the Lord's word
even louder than the train
rattling through the tunnels:
these men in well-tailored suits
obviously on their way
to Wall Street to destroy us;

high school kids in backward
ball caps wearing their backpacks
over one shoulder, high school
for them being anywhere
in the city; guys with beards
and tight jeans wearing sport coats;
secretaries wearing
running shoes and panty hose
with their high heels in their bags;
beautiful Russian ladies
dressed like descendants of czars;
Jewish people moving their lips
reading the Torah, rocking a bit;
women applying product
to their hair right in front of
everyone (which made me think
of a good name for a gel
for hair, "coif syrup")—
all of us waiting down there
for the F train to take us
and soon it came, preceded
by an unnatural gust

of wind from down the tunnel,
turning pages, lifting hair
announcing the imminent
beginning of another
workday, screeching to a stop
opening its doors so packed
at this hour with commuters
none of us bothered to look
for a seat though I always
stood near obvious bankers
who would be getting off soon.
And like many other days
I tried to both hold the bars
and read a new manuscript
before the train delivered
me to Midtown and that day's
editorial meeting
where I would be asked to nod
in agreement with my boss,
Pam, and maybe say something
a little witty making
everyone laugh overmuch

the way they do in meetings,
and for this, not my advanced
degree in literature,
did Pam value me. Sometimes,
though I never got to work on the books
once they were acquired,
Pam questioned me about them.
Which was merely punitive
I complained and my wife said
Well that's why they call it work
so I stood there knee hurting
in a crowded train hanging
on with one hand and holding
the latest manuscript crook'd
in the other arm, this one
a Victorian-era verse autobiography
and possible reprint called
CONFESSIONS OF THE TRULY
HIGH, which title I admit
was intriguing and Pam said
it was being considered
for the new Retrievals list,

which was to feature the lost,
the forgotten, the suppressed
and could you read it tonight?
she'd asked me last night and smiled
the smile that meant *you'll do it*
and I smiled the smile that meant
even though you can make me
do whatever you want to
I can still give you this fake
simmering-with-hatred smile.
And then I didn't read it.
I didn't do anything
special, just didn't work
after I got home from work,
which was my philosophy.
I did something to my knee
apparently, then I slept
unconcerned knowing the train
was the city's largest most
populous and productive
office, with teachers grading
papers, young women in suits
with laptops open typing

furiously, and then me
cradling the loose pages
turning them by blowing them
or doing it with my chin
and, turning past the title
pages, I started to read—

How came I to leave my home
in the Shenandoah Valley
and sail for Paris?

Paris the city that can
confer importance on a man
just saying its name

Thus I was going to be
famous and live frugally there
and stare at the clouds

but being out at sea
for months is horrifying
nothing ever stops

pitching about heaving
up huge mountains of cold water
the nausea lasts

and lasts and the horror
of floating like a bean alone
on death's blue surface

I saw sailors bent over laughing
throw sheep over the stern
to waiting sharks

and when a squall blows up
upon a small wooden ship
you can't imagine

the kind of helplessness
that pours through you and your legs
and you are lucky

if you can stay standing
not me I headed belowdecks
and wet my breeches

when we finally docked
in Le Havre I turned to a fellow
who I knew spoke French

I said *Doesn't Le Havre*
simply mean "the harbor"? He nodded
«*What's your point?*» he said

Only that it's general
like all these French words, the Grand Prix
merely means "the big prize"

«*Yes*» he said «*you speak French?*»
That's not my point I said *These names*
are categories

I wasn't making myself plain
and by that point we had walked down
the gangplank and sate

on the wooden quayside
floating in a cloud while customs
men shuffled papers

From all the surrounding
houses old women leaned over
their railings watching

France seemed various shades
of grey save when punctuated
by someone's red scarf

or a pot of poppies
on a window ledge but Le Havre
was merely the first stop

The customs men showed me
to the station and soon a train
left the coast behind

followed the river Seine
which was wide like a real river
where it met the sea

not imprisoned in bricks
and forced to flow through Paris green
for reasons unknown

Stepping out at the station
I admit I was overwhelmed

by the same colour
of all the buildings by the sky
the beautiful clouds

that seemed to fill every
inch of space above by the dirt
by the Parisians

not seemingly thinking
how glorious that their city
has Roman ruins

by the way they did walk
or ride bicycles and looked great
I was overwhelmed

And when I took my leave
from the men with whom I'd travelled
where was I to go?

I meant to find a room
but didn't speak French so I walked
along the river

And when I saw someone
I inquired about a room
(I spoke a little)

and soon an old lady
led me upstairs to a small room

and I sate alone
and thought *I've made it to Paris
both blue sky and clouds*

And after unpacking
I went to the closest café
for dinner and drinks

and thought—*this will suit me*
while a man played accordion
I had ever so much work

ahead of me if I
were to attain glory
for my great work,

which work I never did, Reader,
which these confessions will explain,
I trust, as they go along

but unhurriedly for
that was the life I was living
dressing in my best

high-collars, fancy pants
and wandering the twisting streets
feeling the cold age

of the ancient buildings
frowning on my American
inexperience

Thus one day still not quite
recovered from my sea voyage
I passed a chemist

whose disreputable
storefront was painted with mystic
symbols I had seen

in my uncle's closet
he being an old Freemason
and a mysterious one

so I thought *He'll dose me*
with some camphor that will stop
my lusting after

Parisian women
and entered—a ceramic bell
tinkled when I did

The shopkeep stared at me
from betwixt vials and tinctures
in a cluttered array,

dusty oilskin packets,
candle nubs, scrolls, old manuscripts,
faded oil paintings,

statues of obscure gods,
ancient very corroded knives
jars full of fluid

the air was close—musty
with the smell of old wet paper
and an acrid smell

This is a chemist's?
I said with my nasal accent
In English he said

«We have all sorts of things
of a palliative nature
from around the globe

You are American
We have drops to cure you of that»
Meaning what? I said

«Meaning your sense of self
can be cracked open and returned
to its rightful state

with one of these» he said
holding up a strange root
«*Or perhaps it's love*

doth disorder you
Mercury can help you with that but take
that business elsewhere

we deal here only with
maladies of a different sort
Let me look at you»

And he came from behind
the cluttered counter, he was short
and had thick glasses

As he peered up at me
I could see his lips were stained black
he smelled like a skunk

I found his attention
uncomfortable I glanced around

He kept staring
at me and humming quietly
the man was shaking

I thought to myself
Am I here seeking this man's help?
And yet I stood still

Finally he stepped back
and rummaging around he took
a small glass vial

It was a pyramid
of leaded glass with a large eye
on every facet

and appeared to be filled
with a resin or tar a large
sticky chunk of it

which stained the glass inside
where it touched—*I've seen this before*
this same pyramid

«*Then you see much my friend*
it is an ancient secret sign»

Surely not that secret
I said—he waved his hand

and said «*It can be seen*
save that it rarely is»

My uncle pretended
all sorts of secrets, Freemason
gibberish and such

I said *that must be it*
«*The Freemasons*» he said «*are a*
body who can trace

their lineage to knights
who crusaded in Palestine
and learned secrets there

Returning to Paris
they built a temple of secrets
under De Molay

and they mustered power
a frightful amount of power—the Pope said
it was from Satan

and accused the Templars
(that is what they were called) of sins
against God and man»

You don't say?
I said—the old man's wicked smile
fixed me like a pin

«It really matters not
All the charges were falsified
to destroy the Knights

It is said they had
a huge horrific brazen head
they called Baphomet

Under his watchful eye
they did swear vengeance
against the Savior

And» and here he whispered
«they urinated on the cross»

What the devil are you driving at?

«In the pyramid vial
is a substance the Knights Templars
brought back from the East»

I looked at it closely
«Hashish—which Hasan-i-Sabbah
gave his assassins

who are a corruption
of Hashishin—hashish eaters»
It made them killers?

I said, not interested
anymore «*No, killing is what
they wanted to do*

this just made them better»
Then it doesn't make you violent?
«*No, it makes you perfect*»

Perfect? Ah then, good day, sir
I said for he seemed a quack
Thank you for your time

And I made to leave
but he cleared his throat «*I believe
we haven't settled*

on this» I said *Come now
what does it really do? I don't
countenance the mystical*

*nonsense of perfection
What will the hashish do for me?
Because the voyage*

over still weighs on me
Some nights I can't sleep I see waves
tower above me

What will it do for me?
He smiled and sate
« *That is for you to learn*

I trust you will feel quite good
but that is just the beginning
After good will come real

You will feel quite real
I urge you to take this right now
for only 90 francs»

And Reader, you may think
this fellow sounds like a criminal
certainly no one

you'd take seriously
but to my shame it sounded grand
I paid him and left

Walking back to my room
in heightened spirits, wondering
what's going to happen

for I had heard of this
in the Shenandoah Valley
I then slowed down

I had no idea
how one ingested this hashish
it looked like a jam

or something you could spread
on toast. I turned around quickly
and retraced my steps

to the strange chemist's shop
but the gate was already down
the trap had been sprung

*

Returning to my quarters
I sate at my table
turning it over

How to even open
the glass pyramid? Turning it
but finding naught

until petulantly
I poked it in one of its eyes
and it clicked open

the room filled with the smell
of a Shenandoah polecat
on an August night

Thinking it was a spread
I speared it with a knife and tried
to smear it on bread

I considered a tincture
like laudanum but had nothing
to dissolve it in

Eventually I slept
and the next day waited outside
the strange chemist's shop

After an hour the gate
lifted and the old man stepped out
«*You have some questions*

about this perfection»
he said. I said *How the devil
is one to take it?*

«*Be not so worried*»
and he closed up his shop leaving
me standing outside

Right that does it I said
Turning on my heel I went home
and ate the whole thing

And thereupon nothing happened
I paced around my room a bit
but I felt nothing

I lay back on my bed
imagining I was perfect
but knew I was not

After half an hour passed
with no change and things no more real
I felt I'd been had

I put on my hat and went out
walking by the Seine
The sky as usual

was like a painting of the sky
and crossing the Pont
Louis-Philippe I saw stairs

down to a lower promenade
where vagabonds sate

imagining no doubt
that they were captains of great ships
as their legs dangled

off cobblestone bulwarks
that came to a point like a prow
cutting the river

But it seemed rather a lark
so I descended to the quai

And I dangled my legs
like a little boy gone fishing
above green water

And I stared at the clouds
and I looked at the green water
how it was stagnant

apple cores and old wigs
and a tapestry floated by
it was all quite nice

I felt grand—I realized
I could stretch out more than I was
so I really stretched

and heard a strange tone
in my ears that was also
answered in my shoulders

Narrowing my eyes
if I wanted to feel cold
I could
           I thought
in my ears
          a strange tone

(that was a valiant bird!)

          winging up
from the water
             duck

    *

that was a duck

*

in the limestone cobbles it
seems as if very small mollusks
left a little trace

*

I feel a little lost
I thought
          it was as if
syrup overflowed my plate
and filled the air

*

I was saying
I feel a little lost
in time

(a gull)

(a river gull)

(what is that)

        *

In one of
those windows I
could have seen Héloïse
and Abélard

        if Time
was not the way
it is
        is there some
overlap

(no answer)

        *

the vagabonds
seem much more
threatening
            in this music

wherefore does it emanate?

        *

I had to stand up
quickly to prove something

        *

I sate back down
the green water
where it divides
beneath my feet
on either side of the quai
shrinking
to a scale
like toys

a chorus
of angels rising up
in glorious song
behind me

*

two ducks glide
soundlessly like a dream
into the green Seine

*

From the sky

*

Suddenly the vagabonds
were up and shouting

*

I stood
the sky bulged a little
everyone was running

*

I had to lean forward
in my body
it was a conveyance
I could hardly control

go!
go!

I shouted
at my conveyance

*

A horrid roaring noise
came at me
from all sides

and I stumbled
down a narrowing
tunnel of vision
towards the stairs
the roaring in my ears
was like unto the sea

*

stumbling towards the staircase
I had to get up
to the bridge
before the tunnel
in front of my eyes
clanged shut

*

Two old men hurried past
and stared at me
and I heard their thoughts
they thought

«Follow us!»

but it was too horrifying

*

I couldn't breathe

*

Hurrying down the cobblestones
I looked down at my arm
and saw it dragging
against the stones
and furthermore
clad in steel
like a knight of old
shooting off sparks
as I hurried away

*

I sate on the staircase
and closed my eyes

(quack of ducks)

(and delightful breeze on my face)

    *

The rushing in my ears
had stopped
        and when I
opened my eyes

      it was a sunny day in Paris

but more than that

it was more real than that

I reached out to touch it
but the day was just

a bit beyond me
          unlike
a normal day
that you're standing right in the middle of

Thus I continued up
the stairs to the bridge
and crossed to the cathedral

hundreds of people
walked in every direction
some sate behind easels
to capture the view

and each of them

          I knew

was a species of transparent
fixture
     they disappeared
into the background

with a wave of my hand
they moved aside

as I did lumber
in my body
across the uneven cobblestones
with a mouth
that felt like mattress ticking
spread out in the sun

*

I had great plans
great plans
I know I had an idea
it was right there
right in the front
of my face but it
evaporated

it moved

like a butterfly

the more I looked for it
it flitted in the sun

*

When I gazed upon the poplar trees
I saw eyes in all the leaves
each tree a million times
gazing upon me

*

I needed something to drink
my tongue had grown
to forty times its normal size
and every bump
every nubbin or bud
on its surface
was as dry as a desert
thus I sate

at a café
tumbling into a chair
and the waiter
came over and said
«Raaaaaawwwwwwwwwwwrrrrrrrr
hsssshhhhhhhhhhhhhhhhh»
Oh no! I said
apparently I was the one speaking

but after I pantomimed
pouring something
into my mouth

the slate was wiped clear

I thought *How came I*
to sit here? I should order
a drink
                    no time had passed

or the opposite was true
when the waiter set down

a coffee and a bottle of wine
on my table
hours later
my shaking hand
put some francs in his hand

*

Nearby a woman played cello
and a man played mandolin

the sound was as
two little clockwork frogs
made of silver
one climbing so delicately
over the other
they may have loved each other
it swelled at times

it was huge
the clouds moved
in a cotillion
to the song

they were much more than real

I pounded the table
then promptly forgot why

    *

This drew the attention
of two men sitting near me
dainty with their coffees
but looking at me
now and again
as I clutched at my shirt
or stifled a cry
I stood up quickly
and crossed the street
and when I tried
to look back casually
they were still looking
      stroking their moustaches
and one opened his mouth
to speak

and though I was a block away
I know what he said
for the wind said it too

*

I walked along the Seine
towards the Tuileries
hoping to find a crêpe
hoping Montgolfier had made
the world's largest crêpe
to carry him into the sky
and that I could eat it

*

A family of ducks
hugged the side
of the river
        and one little chap
hopped out of the water
to walk along the bricks
for a while

and then slid back in
and caught right up
with his mother
as if to say I'm back

(I clapped!)

    *

I was in a small park
the sun was down
hours had gone by

I hadn't been asleep
somehow I had crossed the river
but time was missing

my mind had been snuffed out
like an oil lamp while my body
had wandered around

but unlike when drinking grog
I felt light and clear, an angel
or a talking cloud

The lamplighter walked past
muttering. I brushed myself off
and walked to the Seine

following it back home
letting myself in silently
the stairs made no noise

Was I really a ghost?
Miraculous competence
was mine for a change

Still in my clothes I fell
backwards on my cot and I slept
for nigh on two days

My dreams were as precise
as visions given by angels
but ephemeral

A crow outside my room
was calling me—I threw open
the shutters, so bright

the day and the trees
so clear, I could see each leaf
The old man was right

everything was more real
at that moment I put aside
my desire to do

what I went there to do
and instead I drank a coffee
then went to the shop

The old man wasn't there
so I found a park and stretched out
beneath a large tree

And in its shade day-dreams
and shadows were one

How I would make my way
in Paris when the money went
was a distant concern

I wasn't scared at all
all my life I saw (right then)
had been a race

betwixt one thing
and the next never slowing down
I thought back sadly

to the way I'd behaved
with my friends when younger
acting rather cold

Now with the Knights Templars'
help the world was totally new
and I was starving

I walked along the Seine
flower-hung women were boating
they were beautiful

from the quai some young men pleaded
for them to sail by
(I wanted a glass of claret)

Everything bathed in sun
everyone fairly fainted across
the lawn everyone smiled

Was this not a sign?
This perfect day, Aeolus blowing patterns
across the river?

Beautiful petite red boats
moving not at all amidst fragrant trees
By and by

I thought of the old man
and returned to find him inside
arranging his books

He regarded me not
but held out his hand for the francs
What was there to say?

I looked up. I was at my
stop; with dignity I strode
off the train, and the doors closed.
That was close, I thought, but not
this book. I wondered which
would be the book that made me
miss my stop and I bumped a guy
and didn't say *I'm sorry*
which felt good for a moment
but soon felt like a dick move,
which resolved into feeling
just a few minutes older.
And I rode the moving stairs
into an increasingly
loud increasingly bright glow
from which I again emerged
into a fluorescent bank
of elevators and I
blinked a couple of times and heard

a voice say very clearly
Just get in there and sit down
which was a thing my wife said
so maybe it was her voice
but then, just like every day,
I pushed past that and entered
HarperCollins Publishers
and sat at my desk in my coat
for a little bit too long
because at the moment Pam
wasn't sitting at her desk
cackling and twirling the cord
to the phone and cackling some more.

Eventually I took
off my coat and got to work
going through Pam's messages
and calling back those people
whose requests I could handle,
what trim size is the new book?
If we print a 4-color
cover how much more is it?
I started to fall into

a cloudy gray place inside
so I stood up, rubbed my hands
down the front of my dress pants,
and walked into the break room
for a cup of very strong
very disgusting coffee
that I only drank to feel
something, even just jitters,
and as I stood there, stirring
with my finger the creamer
into the desolate black—
laughing and punching
the air then slapping his knee:
"Hey man what's up?" Barrett held
up his hand for a high five
that I reluctantly high-
fived but almost didn't.
"Not much," I said, shrugging.
"Oh man, that's some funny shit":
I took this to mean the thing
he was laughing at before.
I didn't say anything.
"All right," he said. "Hey, my man,"

and he laid one hand upon
my shoulder, and looked at me.
"You like fantasy stuff right?"
I raised an eyebrow.
"I mean, sci-fi, fantasy
stuff, imaginative stuff."
"Of course,"
I said, "duh." I noticed him
smile. "All right," he said, "check this
idea I got."

        I said,
"You know I don't acquire
books, man. I just work for Pam."
"No, no, man, just listen up.
I got this great book idea,
it's kind of a stoner flick
meets Harry Potter type thing."
"I just told you, right, how there's
no way I can help with this?"
"Yeah man," he said with a frown,
"I heard you. So anyways,
it's about this guy who has
the power to get so high

you can't believe it, but then
in the morning remembers
everything about his dreams."

"He can remember his dreams
after a night of smoking?"
I said. "That's his superpower?"

"Yeah!" he said, laughing.
"It's like, the lamest power
you could ever imagine!"
He wiped a tear from his face.

"It's monumentally dumb,"
I offered, but his head snapped
back and he said,

        "It SEEMS SO,
it seems like a lame power.
But what if—and you find out
incrementally—your friend
who you grew up with and went
to high school with and hung out
with drinking beer in the park

turns out to be some sort of
wizard or magus, you know,
a sorcerer, and he lives
nearby, like a regular
guy you see down at the bar
and everything's cool, you're friends,
and soon he starts having you
back to his place after hours
with some other dudes, to smoke.
And you do, you love to smoke."

"Who are we talking about?"

"The book," he said, "in the book
this is what happens. You smoke
with these guys but every time
you get home you feel something
is a little wrong, missing
maybe, like something inside.
And you think you're losing it
or you should lay off the smoke
and you notice that this guy

keeps asking you to hang out.
And every time you hang out
he's totally cool. He's nice,
and he's always got some beer
and, you know, he's got vinyl,
he's got amazing records."

"So he's amazing," I said.

"He's amazing, but each night
when you get home you feel weak
and you notice the others
are also not looking good.
Everyone, in fact, looks beat
but him, and then the power
comes into play—in your dreams
you realize this so-called friend
is a demonic wizard
who operates in the realm
of dreams like the rest of us
go about our business here.
He's a sorcerer of dreams.

He engages with you there
and does horrible damage,
mystical and otherwise,
to your dreaming self, who limps
through each day, not knowing it,
not understanding what's wrong,
and each night doing battle
in the realm of dreams with him.

I said, "But—"
            "Yes! But!!" he said.
"But the only difference
this time is you remember
his weird, vampiric, dream-time
shenanigans."

            "Wow," I said.
"So what happens?"

Barrett smiled.
"There'd be something
revealed to him in the dream,

a weakness his so-called friend has,
but only glimpsed s o briefly,
and anyone else that high
would never remember it.
But you do, because you can,
because that is your super power."

"What are you talking about,"
I said, "like puzzles
whose solutions he receives
in the dreams? How would that help?"

"Sort of. It's like, in the dreams,
the guy figures out his friend
is really this evil mage
who is like a soul vampire,
and the dreamy psychic pain
has real-life consequences.
So I imagine they all
just start feeling terrible,
they have headaches, hair falls out,
they lose weight, they don't know what

is going on, because they
are too high to remember
their dreams, where all this is clear.
And you know what," Barrett said,
"this shit is not so far out.
I mean, what if all those films
where things happen in our dreams
that actually affect us
was a manifestation
of the scientific truth,
you know, like Niels Bohr said—
'Everything real
is made up of things that can't
be regarded as real.'"

"But the hero remembers?" I said.
"Sure."

I shook my head. He moved past
to get a cup of coffee.

Barrett was essentially
a good guy. Like most people
in publishing—young people—
secretly he wanted to
write books, not track their Return
on Investment. Probably
he wouldn't last very long.
I never saw the older
people I worked with telling
each other excitedly
about a book idea.
I honestly didn't know
how long I'd stay. I saw Pam
swishing in her finery
down the hall and realized
the editorial meeting
was about to start. I said
bye to Barrett and returned
to my desk to get some stuff
to make it look like I cared
about the meeting—notebook,

pens, some random manuscripts.
Pam smiled at me and we walked
to the conference room.

"Did you
read it?" she arched her eyebrows.
"Of course," I said. She gave me
a searching look that was part
interrogation and part
fooling around, then punched me
on the arm and laughed aloud.
"I knew you did! You're the best!
Whatever would I do
without you?" she asked, hugging
me to her with a meaty
arm. I drowned in her perfume.
The smile on my face must have
given me away because
Mark, the big boss, called out, "Pam!
Let the kid breathe," and I thought
Kid? I'm married. Pam let go
and we took our seats around
the conference table. Outside

all that could be seen were more
skyscrapers, other people
in other conference rooms,
in the distance one small cloud
somewhere north up the Hudson.
I imagined a backyard
where a kid playing outside
is suddenly in shadow
for just a moment, and then
the shadow moves on, the cloud
blows past.

       Mark got the meeting
started. All the editorial team
were there, all the bigwigs
and their assistants—Barrett
gave me the thumbs-up across
the table, my friend Lisa
was smirking and doodling.
Going in turn around the table
the editors presented
the week's manuscripts.
There were several proposals

about angels, financial
how-tos, books about dating,
and none of the assistants
had to say a word. Lisa
doodled like she always did.
Barrett made thoughtful faces.
But when Pam's turn came she smiled
tapping the pages against
the table to straighten them,
and announced brightly, "We have
something for the Retrievals
list. Some of you might have read
CONFESSIONS OF AN ENGLISH
OPIUM EATER. Thomas
De Quincey?"

   Some people laughed.
"Some of us went to college,"
she continued, "and trust me,
this is much better than that."
She looked at me.
     "Much better,"
I said.

"First, the narrator
isn't such a pompous ass," she said.
This might be the only thing
I respect her for, I thought.
De Quincey's prose sucks.
"Second, this is about pot."

"Is that as sexy as opium?"
someone asked.
                "It's more modern,"
she said.
"Readers will find this much more
relatable. Opium?
Have you honestly even
smoked it?"
        Barrett and Lisa
winked at me at the same time.
Which I didn't understand.
Pam was still talking. "This book
was in a sense never
published. We only have
a pirated edition

by John Brooks. He famously
pirated Percy Shelley's
QUEEN MAB right here in New York."
Under their breath someone said,
"Famously?"
        "So this, for us,
unique opportunity,
can be spun to demonstrate
our commitment to the past
while we entertain hipsters
today and for years to come."

"Ok, but will they read it?"
Mark tented his fingers, leaned
forward, and smiled. Pam gestured
at me, and because
I either wasn't
listening or didn't care,
I said, "It's in three parts."
No one said anything. Pam
swatted me and said, "Tell them!"
"I think stoners will read it,"

I said. Barrett and Lisa
laughed, and so did some others.
Shuffling some papers, Mark said,
"With that ringing endorsement,
I suggest we get copies
from Pam"—Pam looked at me—"soon,
and we can revisit this
next week." Everyone shuffled
papers before the next item
on the agenda; Mark turned
to Pam and said, "I'm sure it's good."

As soon as it was over
I hurried down the hall, dumped
the manuscripts and notebook,
and ducked into the safety
of the elevator lobby.
It was, traditionally,
too early to go to lunch
but I didn't want to see
Pam right after that meeting
and figured if I could make

the copies and distribute
them to everyone later,
while they were at lunch,
there would be the illusion
of all kinds of thought and care
that might make up for the way
I'd handled myself today.
Also, it was 11:17,
which was not 11:30
(just about the earliest
I could actually go out)
but was within fifteen
minutes of what's permissible.
And my father always said
Never start a job Friday
and this seemed in the same spirit.
When I stepped from the lobby
into the fog of honking
that was everyday Midtown,
having put today's meeting
behind me, my only thought
was a tug-of-war between
street foods—falafel or tacos.

After eating standing there
against an office building
I took a walk to the park
and though I only barely
went in, taking the outer-
most path for the briefest time,
I felt temporarily
elsewhere, and I felt at ease
which feeling also worried me
because I loved living in the city,
but recognized sometimes
this need to retreat, even
into an artificial
retreat, like barely walking
through the park and feeling good.
But I did feel good again,
and I felt that way until
afternoon, leaning over
the cubicle opposite mine
at the end of the hall,
talking to my friend Lisa
about the Thomas Pynchon
novel that had just come out

when I sensed my boss walking
behind me, and then slowing,
and then she pinched me
on the ass. I must have looked
shocked. Lisa's eyes were wide
never leaving mine and when
I didn't turn around
or say anything to my boss, oh then Pam
was furious, the whole room
filled with her fury. She left
down the long hall and Lisa
started to laugh. "What
was that?" she said. "Oh my god
she just pinched your ass
didn't she? She is out of control!"
And she was. My face must have
fallen because Lisa said,
"Oh no, don't take it like that.
Everyone knows it's not you."
"I know, I know, but Jesus,"
I said, sitting on her desk,
"she won't leave me alone,

she never stops. She takes me out
to lunch almost every day.
That's great—I love a free lunch,
sometimes, but not every day.
I just want to read. I want
to think my own thoughts. I want..."
"I know, you want her to leave
you alone."

              "And that's not all.
I *have* to go out with her.
She freaks out if I say no.
I mean it, she freaks out
and starts to cry or storms out.
She makes a huge scene and then
even though I didn't do
anything—it was all her—
is upset because I maybe
have to run an errand or
have lunch with you or Ron."

                        "Oh,
I know! She fucking hates me."
"Well, yes, she does, because you're..."

"Young and cute?"

"Absolutely.
That's exactly why."

"She hates
it if I even ask you work questions."
"I know," I said, "it's true.
She's a jealous old hag."
"But she does have large
breasts," Lisa said.

"Ugh, don't talk
about them, I've seen her use
them at the sales conferences.
Ranieri? You know, that guy
who wrote that marketing book?
I had to sit there while he talked
about them like they were
her children. And she loved it.
It's disgusting."

"That's insane,"
Lisa said. "You have to stop
going out with her."

"I can't.

She took me and my wife out
too—a couple of times. I think
she gets off on it. And then
oh my god this is the worst—
she basically made me stay
in her apartment while she
was out of town. *Your wife
can stay too* she said. My wife can
stay, too? Of course she can stay
too! She's my wife. What the fuck
did she think—I was gonna
sleep in her bed by myself
while my wife stayed home?"
"Holy shit," said Lisa. "You have to
get out of this place,
you know? That is absolute insanity."
"I mentioned how she also makes stuff up
to get mad at me about?
And then forces me to hug
her to make up? It's just like
having a totally fucked-up
relationship at work."

"It is having a fucked-up
relationship at work. Then,
as the cherry on the top
don't forget she just pinched you
on the ass."

                "Oh yes," I said,
"I can still feel that."

                        "You should
take off," she said. "What could she do?"
"Do? She'll make me hug her
for one, then it'll just be
so unpleasant."

                        "You need to go.
I mean really, get out
of here. Just get another job
—or go tell on her."
"Tell on her? You mean HR?"
"Yeah," Lisa said. "I'd hurry."
I thanked Lisa and headed
down the long hall to the bank
of elevators behind
huge glass doors and wondered

what I was about to tell,
down in HR. Everything?
I'd probably have to start
in the abstract or something,
it seemed unlikely that I
was being sexually
harassed. And this was the first
time it had crossed my mind.
Would HarperCollins Publishers
give a shit about a new
assistant who isn't wearing matching
socks? A familiar fog filled
my head as I approached them,
fog of understanding things
were about to go badly:
When I turned the corner
Pam was already in there.
The HR woman looked over
and when she did Pam turned
around, and there was a look
on their faces that made me
turn right around and hurry

across the gray carpeting
to the elevators
when one was just closing up.
I slid in and pretended
not to see Tamara there
behind two bike messengers.
Tamara was probably
on Pam's side—all of them were,
surely, Pam was so high up
she was everybody's boss.
I hurried through the lobby
and turned left on Fifty-Third
past the small public garden
with the waterfall that falls
loudly down a rocky wall
and washes, with its white din,
all thoughts of work from one's head
for the duration of lunch.
I was headed across Sixth Avenue,
to St. Thomas, an Episcopalian
church—beautiful stained glass,
mostly blue, high ceilings,

and that smell of stone and wood
pews and dusty red hymnals
that, though I don't believe, feels
restful. A sanctuary
literally in case Pam
came storming in (my grandpa
baptized me Episcopalian
so my pleas would have to be
honored) (I thought) and candles
added to the smell.
I took a pew on the right
and sat back, and looked around.
Dust seemed to climb up the beams
of stained light that was raking
down from the highest windows.
Behind me a homeless man
fiddled around in his pew.
I looked to see if a priest
or churchy woman would care
whether I read a book there,
or should I put my book
behind a hymnal and read

it that way? No one was there
to see me but the homeless man,
who was really wriggling
now, so I opened my book
and thought to myself: This is
something I never get to do.
I also thought I should
go back to work, but what for?
I was clearly already
unwillingly a part of
a corporate narrative, where
New Guy Who's the Assistant
Gets Fired. I could go
home, but wasn't relishing
another long talk about
Don't you even want a job?
and *How many times are you
going to just walk away?*
So I sat in church
quietly filling my head
with colorful beams of light.
I was pretty sure when he

was young, in seminary,
my grandfather visited
this church and sang in a choir
and saw real opium dens
in Chinatown, which I wished
were still in operation.
My book was small; I took it
from my inside pocket
and stuck it in a red hymnal,
just in case a priest
sneaked up on me while
I was engrossed, which I soon would be,
and opened to the first page
of THE OTHERS, and started.

> The little right-hand drive
> car pulled into the town
> square and stopped in front of
> the only shop. A large
> man with unruly
> white hair got out
> the driver's side and two long-haired

young men got out the other.
Everyone knew they were
students, and foreigners,
and locals' only thought was,
"We will raise the trout's price,"
for to buy a fresh trout
these waters were known for
and pan-fry it in butter
is the reason
most outsiders came here.
It was why these three were here
too. Jake, the one with curly
long black hair, and Brendan,
with absolutely straight
blond hair, and Professor
Baer, had come all the way
from Dublin, where they
were visiting. They had
their small car, three copies
of ULYSSES, and several
cases of cheap red wine.
Jake and Brendan didn't think

much beyond the wine
and the wild western coastline,
so close to the North Sea
they had never seen.
If it seemed strange for them
to travel with this man
they barely knew except
through his seminars
on Joyce and Yeats, they didn't
think or hadn't thought of that,
yet. Soon enough. For now
they stretched their legs and breathed
in the cliff-high sea air.
"I'll get us booze,"
said Baer, "you two pick out
a nice trout from the shop,"
and walked away. Brendan
and Jake smiled. They walked
across the village green
past a nasty-looking statue
of a somber, apparently common
man holding a fishing spear.

Inside the shop, it smelled
of fish and cigarette smoke.
Two men were talking
to a very tall woman
shelving cans. They all looked
around when the bell rang
over the door. Brendan
saw a table of trout
and mussels laid on ice
and walked over to it.
"Yes?" the tall woman said.
"We need a trout," said Jake,
"a nice one."

                    "Well, this one
still writes letters home to his mum,"
the woman said, laughing,
along with the two men.
The American boys
shared a look.
"Sounds perfect. We'll take him."
"And potatoes you'll need,"
the woman said. She held

a paper bag of them
out until Jake took it.
"Do we need these?" he whispered
sideways and Brendan said,
"Let's just take them and go."
And outside in the sun
Brendan took the trout from
its bag, and headfirst
into his back pocket
it went with them.
Professor Baer waited
beside their little car
with a fifth of whiskey
whistling an Irish tune,
and asked, "Where's the trout?"
When Brendan turned around
the professor giggled
in a surprisingly high
birdsong and opened up
the trunk. A shadow raced
across the green and held
steady over the car

until they all noticed
it had gotten darker.
Baer lifted his head out
of the trunk and a little girl
in a long coat stood there
looking quite openly
at the Americans.
"You'll be off to the old
Sullivan place," she said.
"We're off to the island,"
Baer said, smiling at her.
"What's your name, little one?"
"That's the Sullivan place."
Wind began blowing in
from the sea. "Well we spoke
to a Mister Flaherty,"
said Baer, smiling at her.
"It's the Sullivan place
even if they aren't there
anymore," the girl said.
The car was loaded now
and the two boys were in.

"Of course," said Professor Baer,
"the names of things live on."
"Yes, the names live on,"
she said, walking slowly backwards
across the town green.
"What was that all about?"
said Jake as they drove north
towards a distant rusted bridge
connecting the road
to an island so close
it almost seemed pointless
to have a bridge. Baer smiled
at them through the rearview
and put the radio on.
Frantic fiddling.
He hummed along with it.
Brendan said, "Do you know
every Irish ballad?"
And Baer said, "This isn't
a ballad, it's a reel,
a ballad would be slow,"
and loudly, he started

singing a different song:
"*Oh Kitty! My darling*
remember, that the doom
will be mine if I stay."
The little car shuddered
crossing the rusted bridge.
Soon the road swung around
to windward and a small
weathered stone house appeared
from behind tall rocks
that had tumbled down onto
a sandy beach with kelp
strewn around like writing.
"The Sullivans welcome you,"
said Baer. "Don't you feel that?
They were fishermen,
like most people you meet
around here. But they're gone
now. Now we live here."
"For the weekend at least,"
said Brendan, punching Jake
playfully on the arm.

The three of them got out
and walked to the beach.
Clouds filled the western sky
now and the wind picked up.
It was suddenly loud,
as loud as possible,
Brendan thought. Professor
Baer said, "Go get your boots.
It's low tide. And mussels
await those with good boots."
They could have bought mussels
in the shop, but Brendan
stopped grousing about that
after a few minutes
standing in a shallow bay
at low tide picking
clusters of purple-black
mussels from exposed rocks.
The tide kept receding.
Jake and Professor Baer
moved off in different
directions, a light rain

spotting the exposed sand.
Seabirds that were not quite
gulls ceaselessly cried out
like the souls of the damned.
With their plastic bags filled
with mussels and sand
the boys slowly made their way
back to the old stone house,
and stood there, looking out
at the professor bent over
pulling mussels.
The sky was much darker
and the sun, wherever
it was, must have gone down.
"Let's take these in. No way
we can eat it all,"
Jake said. They put them down
in the large porcelain sink
and looked through the house.
The ground floor was mostly kitchen,
a huge hearth, and some chairs.
Upstairs were two bedrooms,

the bathroom, and a fireplace
with what looked like church pews.
Framed pictures on the stairs
of stern, high-buttoned men
and humorless women,
also several photos
of a small fishing boat
all faded and salt-stained.
Not a lamp in the house.
"It's going to get really dark
here tonight," Brendan said.
"It's going to get really drunk
here tonight. Did you see
how much wine old Baer brought?"
said Jake, tossing a box
in the kitchen fireplace.
"Have you ever eaten
mussels?" Brendan asked,
looking slightly worried.
"They're fine. There'll be garlic
and sauce, you won't notice
them. Just eat them quickly,

that's how I deal with things."
Loud drops of rain knocked hard
on the windows and Baer
threw open the front door
grinning and holding up
mussels and a dead shark.
"I'm not eating that,"
Jake said.

                "It's not to eat.
This is a sign of luck."
"Not for the shark," Brendan
said.

        "Luck for our evening,"
said Baer, pulling out teeth
from the rubbery jaws
and handing them to each
of the boys. "Keep these on
you tonight," he told them.
"On us?"

        "In your pockets
is fine."

        "What are they for?"

"I told you, they're for luck."
Soon all three were chopping
garlic, shallots, parsley,
warming up a deep pan.
After dinner beside
a small, rather poor fire
made of strange pressure-packed
bricks of peat, Professor Baer
pulled out of his bag
ULYSSES, a very worn copy,
and started to thumb through it,
humming a disconcerting tune.
Jake opened another
magnum of red wine
and brought it to the fire.
It seemed as if the rain
had stopped, but then a gust
of wind just blew the rain
against the old windows
and the boys each felt wind
actually blowing
down his collar. They

looked at one another
and made just very
slight movements of the eyes
which meant a lot of things.
"We were talking last time
about the ghosts in here,
the spirits, either dead
or somehow fictional,
and in particular
the journey to the Land
of the Dead, while alive,"
said Baer, and shut the book.
A long time seemed to pass.
"Were we talking about that?"
said Jake, wiping a wine ring
from his copy of the book.
Brendan flipped ULYSSES
back and forth, wondering
what Professor Baer
was talking about;
last time their ULYSSES
club met, everyone

got drunk (but thought it
something elfin
and majestical) on absinthe.
No one talked about ghosts.
As far as he knew ghosts
were really only part
of Homer's ODYSSEY
not Joyce's ULYSSES,
but he hadn't read all
of it and was waiting
for the special event
where they read the whole thing
aloud, by the fireplace,
all night long, and he thought
tonight was sure to be that night,
but Professor Baer
seemed to have other ideas.
Baer set down
his copy of the book
and tented his fingers
in front of a half-smile
and waited. No one said

anything; Brendan looked
at Jake, who made a face.
The wind picked up and blew
a wall of rain at them.
Brendan broke the silence.
"What do you mean about
ghosts—are there really ghosts
in this book?"

           "The question
is really, are there ghosts
at all? Anywhere? Here?"
said Baer, sweeping his hands
menacingly around.
The fire went dim all of a sudden
and Jake yawned and stretched
to cover a shudder
he felt rushing up
from the back of his neck.
Brendan coughed. The professor said,
"You two aren't interested
in them? In the Others?"
"Are we talking about ghosts?"

Brendan asked, leaning
forward. The peat fire flared.
"Yes, ghosts, some call them that,
some call them visitors.
I call them the Others,
it's much more accurate.
They are not visiting—"
A loud bump from upstairs
startled the boys, but Baer
kept smiling. "Like I said,
'ghost' is inaccurate."
"Did you hear that?" Jake said.
"Yes," Brendan whispered back.
They looked at each other.
"But how are they NOT ghosts
if they're dead? Why don't you
say what you mean," said Jake.
"Yeah, tell us what all this
is about—all these ghosts
in Joyce or whatever."
Poking the peat fire, Baer
cleared his throat. "I'll tell you

a story. It happened
to me in Paris. Please listen carefully.
What happened to me there
has fundamentally
changed my understanding
of nearly everything."
"When you put it THAT way—"
Jake chortled.

                    "Quiet now,
and listen. The Others
are here too and afterwards
they may make themselves
more apparent to us.
Hold on to those shark teeth.
Here's what happened to me.
I had a job teaching
the Romantic poets
in Paris one winter.
I knew nobody there
but the secretary
of the Literature
Department, and one man

who taught Cubist poets
for whom I have disdain
and so we rarely spoke.
I spent much of my time
wandering around the city,
lost but not minding it,
stopping every few hours
to get French onion soup
or browse through a bookstore.
Paris, still, to this day,
has so many bookstores.
New York, London, they don't
come close. The life of books
is lived so deeply there.
I also remember
one cold night wandering
past an atelier
selling beautiful knives,
very expensive ones,
and behind a window
a young man
slowly grinding bright knives

in a dark studio.
And so, feeling like this—
alone, cold, wandering
around identical
ancient stone streets—I felt
drawn one rainy morning
underground. I wandered
across the Seine, which was
the exact same color
as all the buildings, which,
I'm sure you know, are all
built from the exact same
stone, a quite pale limestone
which they quarried under
the city, leaving miles
and miles of forgotten
tunnels and passages,
some of which, I had heard,
had bacchanalia
in secret, and I thought
I would enjoy doing that,
something secretive.

But it turns out no one
will tell you where they are,
though they're underneath you
at all times, you can't ask
a waiter, like I did,
'How do I get down there
to join the revelry?'
Soon I found myself south
of where I usually went
and saw a discreet sign
to 'Paris Catacombs,'
which I'd only vaguely
heard of. And then I saw
a long line of people
on a small street despite
the very cold weather
and the fog that kept changing
into rain. I stood there
with them, moving slowly
towards a small brick building
where a staircase took us
deep under the city.

We descended stone steps
until the air got warm.
I had quite forgotten
I was claustrophobic.
Hundreds of feet of stone
pressed on me from overhead
and the only way out
was forwards—people kept
coming down behind me.
So I began to walk.
I walked, having to stoop,
through tunnels carved by hand
in dim light, breathing in
hundreds of years of dust.
There was just the tunnel
for a long time, but then
it opened up upon
a forbidding-looking
gateway, with a warning
that we were entering
the Domain of the Dead.
And we were. Right away

the passages were lined
with bones, literally
millions upon millions
of them. It is said
six million skulls are down there,
and I saw every one.
And they aren't just dumped there,
no, the bones have been stacked—
'lovingly' is the word—
and decoratively,
a layer of femurs,
then a layer of skulls—
on and on, everywhere,
lining the walls, ringing
columns in the center
of larger open spaces,
artistically, also
painstakingly arranged,
six million skulls, endless.
It's overpowering
in a way but also,
especially if one

is down there all alone,
one realizes nothing
can be done about it.
Nothing to say, no one
to say it to, one walks
on through the walls of bone
until reaching the end,
happy beyond measure
to have to walk up stairs.
And then, across the street,
a gift shop with death's-heads
on anything you like.
Even the foggy air
was a delight, and soon
I found myself sitting
in an Algerian restaurant
drinking wine
and eating way too much.
And the experience
was over, behind me,
no one else sitting there
had just seen what I'd seen.

Everyone was laughing,
baklava in their mouths,
unaware, unlike me,
of the fact of being
quite alive, filled with wine,
and surrounded by friends.
I made my way back home
and by the time evening
came around I wasn't
thinking about the day
at all. I had to teach
the next day, and I reread
Shelley's Ode to the West Wind,
'O wild West Wind, thou breath
of Autumn's being, thou,'
et cetera. You know it.
And when I went to bed
my mind was on Shelley.
But then I had a dream.
More than a dream. I lived
another life in Paris,
walking the narrow streets,

exactly like my life
while I was awake, but
one huge difference—the dead
were everywhere I went.
Along every street, ghosts
loitered, or went about
their business. They were like
a translucent curtain spread
against every building,
ghosts on every street, ghosts
on ghost bicycles,
ghosts driving in ghost cars,
it might sound humorous
but believe me, this was
more than a dream, it had
a particular sheen.
And then I was approached
by one of them, a ghost
or, now I know, an Other,
who suddenly came up
to me and yelled at me,
shouting, 'Hey! Hey!' and he's

shoving me back, shoving me back,
shouting, 'You've seen enough!'
and then he shoved me out
of the dream, into bed,
the echo of his shout
still in my waking ears."

I closed the book
and turned around. Homeless guy
was rattling his pew.
I looked quickly and then
I looked away. He was
definitely tugging it,
right there in the pew.
I should get out of here,
I thought. And I did.
The sun began to set
on top of Hoboken.
The result was gorgeous.
I stood looking downtown,
Sixth Avenue, the lights
stretching out and rising

upwards on the buildings
emitting a real, a tangible
power, and you can feel it
standing there in New York.
A light breeze also blew,
and it was distracting
me as I pretended
I had not just walked out
on Pam, the terrible,
absolutely awful Pam,
who had beaten me
to Human Resources.
From nowhere, someone's hand
took hold of my shoulder
and I heard my name said.
I turned slowly and saw Ron.
"Ron, what are you doing?"
Ron laid his other hand
on my other shoulder
and said, "I thought you headed
home." I said, "I think I meant to
but didn't make it very far.

Then I sought sanctuary
at a church—I know, I know—
at church, it doesn't make much sense,
but I did it and now
I guess it's time to go."
It seemed like I was high.
What I remember is its not
even being a question
that we'd go to O'Houlihan's pub.
And we ordered Guinnesses.
And there was an awkward
silence and then I coughed.
Then Ron said, "What'd you do,
after you left your desk?"
"I sought sanctuary
in a church my grandpa
had once performed inside,
or been in, or something.
Oh! And I started this book,
do you know it? It's called
THE OTHERS. It's pretty good."
"That's the one about ghosts,"

said Ron. "That book is everywhere.
But is it REALLY good?"
I could tell Ron wanted
to make something of this,
whatever the this was,
so I said, "It's all right."
Then I looked at my friend
and said, "Have you ever
seen one of those, a ghost
or something? a presence?"
Ron finished his Guinness
and said, "I saw a ghost,
for real, in my basement.
I shit you not, a ghost."
"All right, what's the story?"
"Well, as you know, we were,
you and me, as well as
the other guys, a band,
and remember how we,
as a band, had to keep
our band things stored somewhere?
And how it was my place

that had the basement?
Well that meant every time
we're done unloading shit
into the basement
that I had to be the last one
locking up from the inside,
the last one up the stairs,
and even though I never said
a thing to you guys, it scared me
shitless. And I was embarrassed.
But I really did feel
some fucked-up shit down there.
The fucking hairs stood up
on the back of my neck.
I felt ashamed to say anything
about it. Thanks for bringing
it up. Have YOU ever seen one?"

"Wait—THAT's your ghost story?"

"Well, no. I saw something,"
Ron said. "I saw an arm.

A hairy, yellow arm.
It took a swipe at me.
I was running upstairs.
I looked back and saw it."
"Jesus," I said. He said,
"It wasn't real, I think,
but I saw it, for sure.
The image was broadcast
to my brain to see it.
So I saw it. I guess."

"Well, that's not really much
of a ghost story, Ron.
I've actually got one.
Can I tell it to you?"
A young Irish waiter
leaned down in between us
right then and Ron asked her
for two more Guinnesses.
The place had really filled up,
work must have ended
everywhere in Midtown.

"Yes," Ron said, turning back,
"tell me your ghost story."
"Well," I said, "it's not mine
exactly, it happened
to my brother-in-law."

                    "Uh-huh."

Two imperial pints
settled down between us.
Ron waved me off and paid.
"Ok, so this was in Ireland,
actually, weirdly, just like
this book I'm reading.
Anyway, he was there
with a girl, and living
with her in a small house.
And so on the bedpost,
which was metal,
there was a crucifix.
And it made lots of noise
anytime someone moved
the slightest bit in bed.
Which seems a little strange.

But whatever. But then
he started feeling strange
at night, and hearing sounds
that he felt were inside
his head, and he believed
some other force controlled
his thoughts, which he said ran
wild every night, and he
couldn't stop them at all.
So then one night he sees
while he is lying in bed
a black diaphanous
shape rush to the next room.
Just then, this girl wakes up
and says, "I had a dream
that a black figure rushed
right past our bed just there"—
and he said, "That's no dream."

"That was an even worse
ghost story than mine. Plus,"
Ron said, "a ghost story

has to happen to you,
not in the third person."
"Well, it happened," I said.
"I'm sure it did," said Ron.
"But the story works best
if it happened to you."

"I've tried to see them,
I sat up late
in my uncle's attic
waiting, where a young girl
supposedly had died
of tuberculosis,
but she never appeared.
I think ghosts don't like me."

"They're like girls," Ron said. "You're trying
too hard. Plus they're not real."
Soon we ordered wings. Night
fell just past the city.
"I wonder if I have
a job there anymore?"

"I certainly wouldn't come in
tomorrow, either way,
if I were you," he said,
"let everyone cool down.
Also, here's this." He handed me
a manuscript.

            "What is it?"
"It's way better than that
ghost stuff you've been reading.
It's awesome. I think we're pubbing
next spring, but you should check this out now.
You'll love it.
It's a French book about altered states.
It's called L'ENCHANTEUR."
"All right, thanks. I'll read it."
"Just read it now. Don't finish
THE OTHERS," he said.
He looked funny
saying it, his eyes flashed
in the disco ball's light
coming from the back room.
We hugged and he went up

to One Twenty-Fifth Street.
Waiting for the F train,
I turned to the first page.

The man and the woman
who seemed to be camping
on closer inspection
were not campers at all.
They made their way in stealth
between the pine tree trunks
without making a sound.
The man had a gun drawn.
The sun shone down in shafts
sporadically; the trees
were thick on the mountain-
side they climbed. Everything
else in the forest stood
motionless,
or so it seemed to them.
"Extremely worrisome,"
whispered Jacques to Raquel.
"He's not far now," she said,

"the summit's just up there."
"And what else is up there?"
asked Jacques, checking his gun
for pine needles, sliding back
the chamber and blowing on it.
"Well," she said, "you know, thugs,
I guess. Hired goons."
"Louts? Roustabouts?" he said.
"A cast of ne'er-do-wells,"
she said. "Here's where we are."
She held the GPS
device out between them.
Its topographical
layering revealed them
to be two rings under
the summit, near a house
that looked like it might be
an armed compound.
"We should head left,"
he said, straightening up.
He saw Raquel pause,
then he heard it, too: birds,

the soft thunderous
sounds of flapping
wings and birdsong
rising from above them.
He crouched and held the gun
in front of him, shouting
at Raquel, "Hit the deck!"
when, through the trees, two forms
emerged, enormous beasts
ten feet tall, and hairy,
with unnaturally bright
yellow eyes—LEDs,
they'd figure out later.
Jacques fired—once, then many
times. A Ping! Ping! was all
they heard. The beasts kept
charging downhill at them.
"Merde!" Jacques said. "Run!"
screamed Raquel, and they ran
straight down the mountainside.
The beasts were after them.
They were too fast for them.

They had it out for them,
was the last thought Raquel had
as a needle pricked her
behind the right ear
and she stumbled and fell
but never hit the ground.

What she hit was a pit
deep inside her stomach,
a very painful place
in her center that throbbed
slowly, though soon she saw,
through eyes she could barely
open, that it was light
throbbing or flickering,
from very far away,
from high on a ceiling
in an old-fashioned room.
She felt sick and heavy.
She turned her head and saw
Jacques trying to sit up
on a cot beside her.

Moaning and covering
their eyes, they tried to stand.
Nausea knocked them back.
"No, this will never do!"
a deep, masculine voice
purred at them. "Please, lie back
and relax, I regret this
unfortunate drugging.
Drugs are so heavenly
when one uses them well."
A short black man
stepped into the room
smiling, spreading his arms
wide in benediction.
"Guillaume!" Jacques sort of moaned.
"Robert Guillaume," he smiled,
"though my friends call me
Guillaume the Enchanter.
Madame," he said, holding
out a hand to Raquel
and pulling her slowly
to her feet. "Allow me

to show you to your rooms."
Guillaume held Raquel up
and Jacques stumbled behind.
They walked down a long hall
lined with windows looking
out onto the forest.
The sun had just gone down.
A few people in robes
walked slowly down a path.
"Your room is here," he said.
"If you need anything
ring the bell by the door.
Soup will be sent up soon.
We will talk tomorrow."
They collapsed on their beds.
"What were those fucking things?"
"They were bigfoots, Raquel.
Robot bigfoots. I shot
them and they just went Ping."
"I guess that explains a lot,"
whispered Raquel, falling
asleep as she said it.

In the morning, coffee
and a plate of bright green
fruits sat on their dresser,
the coffee still steaming.
They each drank a little.
Guillaume entered, smiling,
dressed in a long white robe.
In his arms he held more.
"You'll be more comfortable
in these. Please put them on.
I will see you downstairs."
Downstairs, feeling stupid,
standing there in white robes,
they noticed others too
in robes sort of gliding
through a crumbling cloister,
quince trees in the garden.
"Jacques, Raquel,"
Robert Guillaume announced,
and when they turned around
they both swore (and confirmed
with each other later)

that Guillaume seemed to step off
something they couldn't see
in the air, or he shrank
suddenly as they turned;
neither of these options
fit neatly in their minds.
Raquel opened her mouth;
Guillaume held up his hand.
"I know who you are,
I know why you're here.
No, no!" Jacques tried to speak.
"I know. But, I don't judge.
I want to welcome you
to *ma belle collection*."
They looked at each other,
not because of the French,
of course, they were both French,
and Guillaume beckoned them
across the quince garden
to the cloister's far side.
He turned to look at them
and to speak. Crows flew up

and interrupted him.
"So you are here," he said,
"because I am Terror.
I am literally
the essence of Terror
to you crazy people,
such that you came up here,
up my mountain,
to what? Neutralize me?
All because I love drugs,
lovely, wonderful drugs.
But you don't understand,
none of you do. The drugs
are better than we are.
We're just here to use them,
to keep propagating
all of them. Every drug
out there is using us,
not the other way around.
And if that's not a reason
to start a little cult
then I don't know what is!"

He huffed and thrust his chin in the air.
"Well," said Jacques, "I really
am not sure what to say.
I did not expect that.
I don't think Raquel did,
either, and I just think
we should slow everything
down here, and just kind of,
kind of"—and Raquel said,
"Oh my god, are you high?"
And Jacques said, "Of course not!
What would make you say that?"
And Raquel said, "Because
I am totally high!
You don't know? He drugged us!
We're drugged! We're fucking drugged!"
running through the garden
for a while, muttering,
hands on her head, "Drugged! Drugged!"
"Is this thing true, Guillaume?"
said Jacques, feeling about
five minutes behind.

"Oh yes," he said, "quite drugged.
And soon you, too, will stay
with me, on my mountain,
where you will learn so much
the straight world can't teach you."
"What is your plan, Guillaume?"
"My plan is to convince
in the only real way—
direct experience.
I have argued with words,
music, images—produced
film after film, albums,
masterminded movements
in art and music. All,"
he said, making a fist,
"to convince the straight world
of the drugs' true power.
Nothing has worked. Now you
will feel it—the power
and the revelation.
They will listen to you."
Raquel snorted,

"Do you really think they'll believe
us? They'll just think
we're high, two more messes
who've been duped by your lies.
You don't understand them.
They already believe
everything they want to.
You're wasting your time."
"Yeah, and ours," Jacques added.
"We shall see. You may change
your tune. Please follow me."
He led them out beyond
the walls of the cloister
down a path that skirted
the edge of the forest.
They heard some loud crashing
in the trees and Raquel said,
"So, those were robots?
Those were robot bigfoots?"
Instead of answering,
Guillaume called out something
sounding something like Basque,

and two enormous beasts
stepped out of the trees
and stood at attention
close by. From them came
a very low humming
and the smell of hot metal.
Up close, the creatures' eyes
were even brighter yellow,
much too yellow,
and staring straight ahead.
"Aren't they just marvelous?"
"Uh-huh. What are their names?"
Jacques said, staring. Raquel
punched him hard in the arm.
Her hand felt like it pushed
through his arm and emerged
in a cold, tingling void
where it started to freeze.
She looked closely at it.
A vociferating crow
in one of the trees
was making fun of her.

When she slowly turned back
to face Jacques and Guillaume
she felt as if she'd been gone
for hours. Jacques was waving
his hands in front of the beasts,
saying, "Remarkable,
you're in total control
of them. Also what's up
with their on-and-off eyes?"

At this exact moment
the subway train came up
from the underground. The light
went from fluorescent to tempered,
giving way to darkness
mostly, and to the city's
various pinprick glimmers.
I put down L'ENCHANTEUR
and gazed out the windows
at the harbor,
blackness, and lights from boats.
People started calling

their loved ones to tell them
they'd be home in minutes.
Some phones rang. I looked
at the manuscript and frowned.
Was Ron messing with me?
Did he really like this book?
Where could it go from there?
Didn't the Six Million Dollar Man
have a plotline where he fights
Bigfoot, who's also a robot?
What's going to happen
tomorrow? Will I go
to my job? Will they let me
inside the building?
What's going to happen
when I get home and tell
my wife about my day?
Will I actually use
"sexual harassment"
to describe what happened?
These and other questions
occupied me until

the train went underground
again. I gathered up my stuff
and stood by the train doors
waiting, with the others.

But something
was going to change
when I got home
and had to talk
about Pam and HR
and do, essentially,
what I have done several
times since moving here,
which is realize that work
gets in the way. Or that
I could make no money
without also having
to participate
in abusive role-playing
where emotional pain
is everyone's real boss.
And I unfairly

describe my wife
as writing me off.
She's my wife;
no one understands me
better. I held those thoughts
in front of me walking
upstairs, from the station
into cool night air.
The lights on the marquee
at the movie theater
were especially crisp.
One lone, low cloud blew by,
its presence revealing
just how empty and black
the sky really was then.
My mind was wandering,
and soon I was walking
up our stoop, keys in hand.
I tried to take my shoes
and coat off quietly
so I could surprise her,
mildly. It wasn't much

of a surprise—she knew
I'd be home—but it was
one of love's little
flowerings: a gentle
surprise on someone's face.
I crept up the dark stairs.
Most of the lights were off.
In a pale blue flicker
she sat on our old couch,
legs tucked underneath her.
I bent down and kissed her
on the top of her head.
She smiled at me. Her eyes
seemed huge and watery.
"What's this?" I said, laughing.
"You've had a little wine
I see," I said. She said,
"Not enough. Did you bring
anything home with you?"
"I brought some crazy news
and I will get us beer."
I took them from the fridge

and sat down next to her.
"Something kind of happened
with Pam today at work."
"Oh my god! I know what
it is—part of your job
description from now on
is you're married to her?
Or Mondays are Kissing
Mondays now, is that it?"
"Well, yes, of course, that too,
but a line was crossed
today, the line where she
pinches my ass walking
behind me while Lisa's
talking to me."

                    "Shut!
                    Up!"
she yelled. "No way! Really?
She pinched your ass? Oh no."
She was sitting up now,
looking much more focused.
"Lisa saw the whole thing."

"So what did you do?"
"Lisa told me to go
report her to HR."
"Holy shit. So did you?"
"Well, kind of," I said.
"I went to HR but she
was already down there."
"And then?"
"I just left.
I sought sanctuary
in that church my grandpa
used to do something at,
and then the day was done.
But what about your day?
Why so drunk?"

        "You can't change
the subject just like that."
"How about like this?" I said,
kissing her.

        "What will you do
tomorrow? Can you go back?
What do you think

she said at HR?"
"I'm sure she made some shit
up about me. It's Pam.
She's the boss. Whatever
she says they're going
to believe her, and they'll do
whatever she tells them."
For a moment the look
in my wife's eyes confused me,
then I recognized it
as pity. Sweet pity
I was thrilled to accept.
"Oh sweetie," she hugged me.
"I think you have to go
in tomorrow and quit."
"Ok," I said. "Sure thing."
I couldn't believe it.
She was telling me to.
"If you see her, don't talk
to her. Go to HR."
"Should I even bother
telling them about her,

about all the abuse?"
"It won't matter, even
if they believe you.
Just quit. It's over.
Come to my job and hide
under my desk and kiss
my knees all day long."
"That's a good job for me."
I couldn't believe it.
She wasn't at all mad.
It seemed the right time
to quietly move on.
"So, what are you watching?"
I know I should have asked
about her day but then
we'd still be way too close
to my day, and what-next
for me. "Oh, I don't know,
it just started, BASHFUL,
I think it's called. It's good."
"Is this what we're doing
now?" I asked, opening

my beer. "Catch me up."
The sound had been turned off
for the commercials,
and she said, "Ok. Real quick
before it starts again:
there are these schoolkids,
they were waiting around
for a flight for a long time,
long enough to learn
that Makua, who's shy,
is not a citizen
and everyone else is,
and this takes place somewhere . . ."
"In the future?"

                "Maybe.
A not-too-distant one,
where it's all about who
is a citizen and who
isn't a citizen, I guess.
And so this other guy,
Paishon, was teasing him
about his parentage,

but it's clear Makua
is the protagonist,
and we're supposed to feel
sorry for him. Meanwhile
Paishon is a big jerk
and all his friends
just do what he says,
and they tease Makua
and call him a Separatist,
which he hates,
because he says they killed
his parents, and he cried,
and this girl named Maka
who was with Paishon's crowd
secretly came over
to him and she told him
don't let it bother him."
"Wait—first, where is this place?
What's with the names? Second,
all this happened waiting
for a plane? Are they on
it yet? How much setup
is there?"

"Hold your horses.
They have those names because
it's some island nation
and after the setup
they all got on the plane
even though there were cuts
to scenes of important
serious-looking guys
talking about some threats
from the Separatists.
And so they're on the plane
and it's really intense.
Some unmarked fighter planes
start flying alongside
their plane, and everyone's
freaking out and screaming
and the flight attendants
can't get them to calm down,
it's totally apeshit."
"What happens?"
                    "Suddenly
there's a huge boom and flames
and then a commercial.

Then, when it comes back on,
you see airplane pieces
washing up on a beach
and dead bodies, and then
a couple people struggle
out of the surf to shore.
So basically only
a few people survived
and it just so happens
that they are all children
from this doomed high school trip."
"Wait, is this just LORD
OF THE FLIES all over?"
"It's totally different.
Right away some old guy
finds them, he's like a monk
or something. The plane crash
drew him. He helped the kids
and convinced them to come
into the jungle
where they wouldn't be seen."
"By who?"

"He didn't say
but I assume the guys
who shot down their airplane."
"Is that where we are now?"
"Basically. The monk guy
told them to wait while he
went off to check on things,
and Paishon and his friends
kept trying to contact
home on their devices—
except for Maka, who said
guys, come on, it's hopeless,
they're wet, we're out of range,
et cetera, and then
a commercial, and now—"
and she pointed to the TV.

The show started
and the monk-looking guy
came back to the schoolkids
and paused, and frowned at them.
"You are lucky those things

don't work. The Separatists
would have intercepted
your signals and been here
already. Put them down."
Paishon reluctantly
dropped his device, as did
his three friends. I assumed
the one girl was Maka.
[Is that Maka?]
[Yes, you don't introduce
someone in the setup
and then just kill them off.]
Makua, I figured,
was standing by himself.
The monk guy, whom you learn
later they call Bashful,
so I'll call him that now,
motioned to them to crouch
and, crouching, to follow
him into the jungle.
Paishon first, Makua last—
I felt I'd seen this

before. The jungle rose
quickly and the children
were soon panting and wet
with sweat, while Bashful kept
crawling slowly forwards.
Soon they came to a stop
and Bashful pointed out
three small flowers, pink ones,
by the side of the trail.
"Mountain orchids," he said,
"very rare, except here.
Every spring I see them.
Nowhere else. Follow me."
And he crawled on. The kids
moaned and wiped their faces.
"We're thirsty," Paishon said.
"Yeah, we're starving," his friend
said, halting. "We need food."
Bashful, without turning,
said again to follow him.
In a while they came out
on a rocky outcropping

overlooking the beach. Wreckage, smoke, and bodies were everywhere. Bashful motioned to them to stay out of sight and he peered at the island below. On the left was the beach and a coastline that stretched for miles. Jungle mountains made up most of the rest, and the particular mountain they'd started up was enormous—so high up they couldn't hear waves, just a constant background of chirping, trills, and hoots from the trees around them. "Where are you taking us?" whined one of the children. "Yeah, where even are we?" Paishon asked. Bashful shushed them. Three small black planes

flew over the wreckage,
much lower than they were.
"Oh my god," Maka cried,
sobbing into her hands.
A few moments later
several low booms—
the jets had strafed the beach.
"They really want you dead,"
Bashful said. "I know them.
They will follow you here.
Your only hope is me."
[He doesn't seem bashful.]
[Shhh.]
"What are we going to do?
Where are you taking us?"
Bashful looked at the sky
then he looked down the valley.
"I am not alone here.
You are not alone here."
Overhead, a loud crash
while a monkey passed by
in the treetops.

"Say more,"
said Makua. It was
the first thing I'd heard him
say so far. "Who owns this
island? Do Separatists?
Or are they attacking
an outpost of Homeland?"
"Homeland does have a base
here," Bashful said. "I think
that is not the safest
place for you. I'm taking
you all to real safety.
Come now. No more questions."
He shook a small fruit tree
and dozens of green fruits
fell around them. "Eat these,"
he said. "Very juicy."

A commercial came on,
one for a new device.
My wife got up to pee.
There was a little wine

left, I quickly drank it
right from the bottle.
The show started up again.
"What did I miss?" she said.

Bashful and the children
had emerged from the trees
near a rocky summit.
From the denuded mountain-
top rose tall, narrow limestone
spires that could have been
placed there, so evenly
were they set around
a deep black hole.
Bashful stepped to the edge
of the summit and looked
down. "Are they after us?"
Paishon asked.

"They are here,"
he said. The sounds of men
crashing through the jungle.
The kids sank to their knees.

Bashful pointed across
the sea, to an island
a few miles away. "There,"
he said, "you will be safe."
"But how we gonna get there?"
one of the kids shouted.
"They're coming," Makua said,
trembling and crying.
"Stand up! Into the hole!"
said Bashful, pointing
into the blackness.
"Follow the path through there.
No more questions."
Bashful shoved them forward
towards the dark opening.
They saw a lightly worn
path disappear below
the surface. They climbed down
out of sight. Maka looked
back, just peering over
the hole's lip, but Bashful
had disappeared. Soldiers

swarmed the summit, pointing
their guns and calling out
in tones quite menacing,
but the children were gone,
already far underground
moving forward quickly
as they could in dim light.
After a few minutes
Paishon held up his hand
and everyone halted.
"What can you see, Nene?"
Now I knew one of them
was named Nene. Nene
(the taller one) stepped up
and peered into the dark.
"It continues down, steep."
[Did they establish
his excellent vision,
before?] [Shhh!]
The children
were arguing. Nene
was squinting and peering

down into the darkness.
"Is there some kind of light?
How can we continue
in the dark? This surface
light is going to fade soon."
Makua cleared his throat.
"I still have my device,"
he said. "It has a light."
"Tree, grab it," Paishon said
to the other kid,
but Makua stepped back,
defiant, staring at him.
"It's his device," Maka said,
"he can lead the way."
"Hold on," said Tree. "You think
this tunnel actually
goes under the ocean?
And goes to that island?
Are you crazy?
There's no way that's the case."
"And even if it is," Nene said,
"there's no way that light

will last so long."
"So what are you saying?"
said Maka. "Let's go back
up to the Separatists
and just turn ourselves in?"
A small light, but a light,
flashed on, and Makua
said quietly, "Let's go,"
pushing past them, down, down,
into the former dark.

Maka followed. Nene
looked at Paishon and Tree,
and, reluctantly, they
followed Makua and Maka.
The scene lasted almost
two minutes—a swaying
light moving deeper down.

Then the door-buzzer buzzed.
"Just ignore it."

    "Really?"

"They'll go away." Again
the buzzer buzzed. My wife
sighed and pressed the button
to listen. "Who is it?"
"It's Pearson, from Porlock!"
Cheery sounding even
through the tiny speaker.
"Pearson. Ok. Let him
in," I sighed, turning off
the TV show.
"Pearson," we said. "Welcome
back." He had some whiskey.
"Great, I'll get some glasses."
"Pearson," my wife said, "why,
every time you show up,
do you announce yourself
'Pearson from Porlock'?"
"Because I'm always interrupting
something, ruining it,
generally being
unwanted."
                    "That's not true!"

I said, back with the cups.

"I don't get it," she said.

"When Coleridge wrote Kubla
Khan, it all came to him,
it was an opium vision,
and when he tried
writing it, a person
from Porlock came calling,
interrupting his flow.
I probably just did the same
thing to you guys, right?"

We both laughed.

"How was Michigan anyway?"

"Great," gulping his whiskey.

"I stopped by Ann Arbor."

"Spend time at the Old Town?"

"Of course. The Brown Jug, too."

"Did you just go for fun?"
said my wife.

         "No, family.
My brother got a house
on a lake. Alpena."

With one hand he pointed
to a spot near the top
of his other hand. "Here."
"It sounds nice," my wife said.
"It was awesome. We saw
so many stars! Crazy
stars. My nephew knows all
of the constellations.
And there was a little dock,
it was so dark out there.
The Milky Way, shooting
stars, we saw everything."
"Sounds awesome."
"But you guys!"
he shouted, suddenly
leaning forward. "You guys!
You'll never fucking guess
what happened!"
                    "What happened?"
"This is going to sound crazy,
but Lady and I went—"
"Who's Lady?"

"My brother's dog. She's great.
So we went
out to this old lighthouse.
They were about to close.
First you get to this
lighthouse museum
and Lady's tied outside
and soon I hear whimpers
and her hair is standing
on end when I go out
there. I try to calm her
but she's agitated, trembling,
then the woman comes out—"
"What woman?"
"From the museum.
And she says, *She feels him*.
And I say, She feels who?
It's the lighthouse keeper.
He's there, and she points up
to a light in a room
near the top of the lighthouse.
There's no electricity

there, she says, and I'm like, what?
There's literally none
going to the lighthouse.
Then what's going on there,
I ask her, and she says,
A ghost
is up there, a keeper
who used to work up there.
And check this out—one night
his family was sailing
back home from Port Huron
in a storm, heavy winds,
and he's up there, when Boom!
The power lines go down
and the lighthouse goes dark.
Then, of course, his family
founders, and the boat sinks.
Everyone dies. He freaks
and jumps from the lighthouse.
Then eventually
years later they shut down
the lighthouse but sometimes

even though the power
has been cut off the lights
are on all night.
The woman said, *Follow me*,
and she led me there
and the whole time Lady
is shaking.
The sun's gone down, the light
is that kind of magic light
that feels like something you touch,
and totally silent,
no birds, the wind had dropped.
Down a shaded dirt path
past War of 1812 stuff
like cannons, gibbets,
stocks, a real creepy vibe.
Still silent, and getting
darker so you can see
the light disappearing
from around you. Lady
was growling the whole time.
Just before a hollow

where it was already
dark, like it was night there
already, the woman
said, *It's just up ahead*,
and went back to the museum.
Left us
on this dark path and split.
Lady started whining.
Her fur bristling.
She's sort of backing up.
Probably I should have
heeded her animal
instincts. But that's what's weird
about dogs—even if
they know something is bad
they'll obey their master."
"But she's your brother's dog,"
my wife said.

           "Well, she knows
we're related, I think.
And she's dying
of fright, but I said *come girl*,

and she's begrudging
about it, but she comes.
We walk through the hollow
and it's pitch-dark in there.
Then the path comes right out
on the dunes, and beach grass
is blowing in the wind
off Lake Huron. It's eerie
out there on the dunes
and the lighthouse is there—
classic, black and white striped.
Now it's like a different
day, the wind is so loud
here, and also, I mean,
guys, here's the crazy thing,
there's this other sound,
a really low humming
coming from the lighthouse."
"Maybe it was the wind
blowing through some open
window or crack or something,"
I said, pouring more drinks.

"No, it's hard to explain.
I sort of felt this sound
underneath the real sound
of the wind. And Lady
looks terrified—ears back,
her eyes rolling with fear.
She really doesn't want
to go any closer,
but I feel drawn to it.
And the light was still on
on top of the lighthouse.
The woman swore power
lines had been cut years ago.
But of course, obviously
electricity still
worked there. I guess I thought
I'd figure it all out.
Lady and I got close
with the lighthouse looming
over us. I felt like
it was just watching us
approach, and I heard it

even more clearly then,
this low humming, and then
a really high-pitched sound
on top of that.
It's not the wind.
We start walking around
the base of the lighthouse
and there's a loud cracking
sound. I'm feeling really
freaked out at this point
and then I see it's
the front door, banging in
the wind. I hold it open.
I peek inside and look
up the spiral staircase
and see a faint light.
Lady barks like crazy
and won't follow me in.
I say, *It's ok girl.*
I'm just going to see
what's going on up there.
Lady won't follow me.

So I tie her outside
and start upstairs. She barks
like crazy the whole time.
And the door is banging.
At first I thought maybe
the lighthouse was also
part of the museum,
but quickly it's quite clear
that no one's been in there
for a very long time.
Cobwebs everywhere.
And nitre on the walls,
you know, from Poe's stories,
that white stuff in dungeons?
And as I walk upstairs
I realize I'm crunching
something beneath my feet.
Little animal bones.
Little bones everywhere.
Then I noticed
the super eerie
horror-movie humming

was louder—and moving
downwards
through the lighthouse staircase.
It came down from above.
I kept walking through webs,
I was covered with them.
And here's where . . . I don't know,"
he said, leaning forward
and pouring a huge drink,
gulping most of it down.
"I never made it there."
"You mean you stopped climbing
the stairs?" my wife asked him.
I suddenly noticed
how quiet it was,
like a little bubble
of silence had settled
on us.

   "No," Pearson said,
"I just never made it
up there. I kept walking
and walking. Lots more webs

getting all over me.
I was getting tired,
I could feel my hand move
along the railing,
but I never got there."
A few moments of silence.
"But, I don't understand,"
I said.

"Neither do I,"
he said.

"You mean you stopped
going up, you gave up?"
"Sure, eventually.
But check this out. I looked
at my watch, I thought
literally maybe time
wasn't passing, and then
when I checked it again
it had been ten minutes.
But the lighthouse wasn't
that big—in ten minutes
anyone easily

would have made it up there."
The silence outside tore
open slightly, a car
slowly drove down the street.
I realized I had heard
nothing but Pearson's voice
for the last few minutes.
"That is crazy,"
said my wife.

         "And that's it,"
said Pearson. "I went down.
Lady and I went back
along the now really dark
path, to the museum, which was
closed. All the lights were off.
My car was all alone
in the dark parking lot.
It was like nothing had happened.
Anyway," he stood up.
"I've got to go. Keep it,"
he meant the almost-gone
bottle. He stumbled out.

My wife and I just looked
at each other.
"What do you think about
that story?" I said.
"I think it's a Pearson
story. Another one."
"Do you believe it's real?"
"I have no idea."
I cleared the drinks away
and went to the bathroom.
When I came back, BASHFUL
was on again. Clearly
we had missed most of it:

> Makua's face stared out
> from a cockpit
> wearing a microphone
> headset and grimacing.
> Explosions rocked and flashed.
> Makua barked orders.
> Maka's voice and static.
> Makua was driving

an enormous walker
that looked like a robot;
the cockpit was its face
and Makua controlled
its arms and legs with his,
running in place, pumping
his arms, sweating, yelling
at Maka. There were five
of these huge man-walkers
crashing through the jungle.
Overhead, some black jets
seemed to be air support.
The jets and the walkers
fired into a valley
where Homeland forces hid,
presumably. Maka's
walker-thing reached behind
its back and unfastened
some kind of bomb and tossed
it into the valley.
The huge explosion knocked
all the walkers over.

Smoke filled the air above
all the devastation,
and when it cleared, Bashful
appeared, rising above
the trees, enormous—
he must have been fifty
feet tall. An evil laugh.
Slowly the five drivers began
crawling out of their knocked-down
walkers while huge Bashful
crossed his arms and bellowed.
Bashful's eyes glowed purple
as he laughed then two beams
shot out, melting Paishon's
walker while he was still
partway in it. He screamed
as it puddled around him.
Extremely gruesome.
Bashful kept on laughing.
One of the black jets fired
two missiles at Bashful,
whose eye-beams melted them,

then melted the black jet.
The four kids hid behind
tall limestone pillars
and frantically conferred.
Makua, who now seemed
to be the natural leader,
handed Maka, Tree, and Nene
grenades. Maka kissed him
quickly. "Will these make
a difference?" Nene asked.
"I doubt it," Makua said,
frowning. "But they're
a diversion."
"What are you gonna do?"
The top of a pillar
splintered and fell
around them. A terrible laugh
filled the air. "All I know,"
said Makua, "is he
got diabolical
and mysterious strength
when that strange purple bird

he fought pecked out his eyes."
"Makua," said Maka,
"don't do this." "I have to.
You guys go. Buy some time."
Reluctantly, Nene,
Tree, and Maka slipped off
to confront a giant
guy who they used to think
was a monk, with grenades.
Makua turned and ran
up the slope, through the trees.
He pulled down a visor
over his eyes. The scene
switched to his point of view.
The thermal signatures
of the jungle creatures
lit up digitally.
Information moving
confusingly across
the visor's screen. The sound
of his heavy breathing.
Explosions and screaming.

Makua looked around
erratically, frantically,
his breathing speeding up.
Then he saw it.
The small, harmless-looking
purple bird, staring back
at him. He watched it come
towards him, hopping, cocking
its head, opening
its unusual beak
and then snapping it closed.
He lifted the visor.
The bird hopping towards him.
Another explosion.
Many voices shouting
somewhere in the valley.
The purple bird hopped on
Makua's outstretched arm
and opened its beak.
Whatever was going
to happen to Makua now,
whatever diabolical

change that might save the day,
it was clear he
was terrified. He looked
back and I knew he wished
he were with the others.

Then we went to bed, and lying there
I said, "I didn't ask you
about your day. What happened?
When I came home you seemed—"
                              "Drunk?"
"Well, there wasn't much wine left."

"Hey you would have needed it
too if you'd spent your whole day
having to read books about
the Maréchal de Rais, Gilles
de Laval, from the fifteenth century.
Who was a sick, murderous
wizard or necromancer
who was really horrible,
which was a depressing way

to spend the day, so I came
home and thought we could both drink
the wine, but—where were you?   ·
So I waited then drank it."

"I know, I know, I'm sorry
I didn't call, I was freaked
out about Pam and lost track
of things, you know, then I sought
sanctuary . . ."
                    "Yes, I know
in some church of your grandpa's."

"Yes, and I'm sorry tonight
had to be all about me."
"There was a lot of Pearson
in it, too," she said.
                    I said,
"So what was so bad about
this Gilles de Laval? He did
black magic? What's that even
mean, practically speaking?"

"Oh god," she said. "Alchemy.
I hope I never have to
read any more about it."

"I'm sorry, are you saying
alchemy is black magic?"

"What, are you an alchemist
or something? Of course it's black,
basically all magic is.
All the good things that happen
are supposed to come from God."

"Are you sure? There were never
magicians who were holy?
What about prophets and guys
who lived in caves and saw things?"

"You mean the Desert Fathers,
and they were all in with God."

"Ok, tell me, what's so awful
with all of these alchemists?"

My wife worked at a small press
that published simplified guides
to important ideas.
Last month it was Ouija boards.
MK ULTRA, government
crimes, false flag conspiracies
like Operation Northwoods:
all of these things occupied
her life and helped us pay rent.

"When you think of alchemy,"
she said, "it's not just about
making gold. What they wanted
was total transformation.
They talked about making gold,
but the Philosopher's Stone
was really about living
forever. The search for gold
was just for the amateurs.
And it was those amateurs
who ended up performing
confidence tricks and flimflams
for the credulous," she said.

"That was always only part
of what the Philosopher's
Stone mania was about.
Obviously everyone
loves gold, but there were darker
motives. The Philosopher's
Stone was also supposed to
give eternal life and stop
you from aging. And of course
if this had been meant to be,
according to them at least,
God would make it possible.
Which they noticed he hadn't.
So the very search for it
was considered demonic.
And alchemists were punished
by the Church if discovered.
A partial explanation
of alchemists' secrecy,
but the darker reason was"—
and here she took a long sip
from a bottle of water

she always kept by our bed
—"the truly awful nonsense
they thought would produce the stone.
Albertus Magnus was one,
a Dominican who taught
Thomas Aquinas—they both
pursued every known science
but gave special attention
to alchemy and occult
pursuits. One alleged feat
was the animation of
a brazen statue which then
could speak and was their servant.
But apparently it talked
too much, until Aquinas
became enraged and smashed it.
Nobody knows what they used
to pull that off, and they were
supposed to be holy men,
but the pursuit of the stone
led alchemists to dabble
in the genuine dark arts.

Human blood was often used,
and the worst of all, the fat
from a newborn. A baby."

"Why did they keep doing it
without any success?"

"I think that's a question for
psychologists. It's something
innate, to pursue a goal
so magnificent, and think
everyone before you
has been unworthy of it.
And since every single spell
and experiment they did
was so insanely complex
it was easy to convince
themselves they had merely poured
in the wrong amount of blood
or failed to correctly say
the enchantment. Doing it wrong
was always an excuse.
Plus the sources for these things

were obscure Egyptian texts
and odd interpretations
of Old Testament stories.
Alchemists actually
believed Moses could make gold
and this explains the golden
calf story from Exodus.
Or the Philosopher's Stone
was how Noah lived so long.
But of course they were guessing,
they were like the worst readers
in that way, finding insane
hidden meanings and symbols
in texts and basing their spells
on completely personal
surmising or misreading."

"But what about this French guy?
He seems to have upset you."

"Ugh, the Maréchal de Rais,
he was absolutely vile.
So rich and spoiled and obsessed

with himself and staying young
that he became a monster.
Ever since he was a child
his every whim and passion
was gratified. His castle
had its very own bishop.
He regularly roasted
enough meat for 500
guests, and he had his own troupe
of dancing girls and actors.
Unfortunately he was
what they called learnèd, he read
everything, and anyone
who met with him left feeling
they'd just chatted with the most
astounding mind in the realm.
But he was a monster.
Soon young children from
nearby started going
missing, lots and lots of them,
and eventually some
were traced back to Laval's castle,

and that was the very last
place they were seen. So many
kids started disappearing
that parents started telling
them to steer clear of his place,
and the children themselves told
stories of Laval as if
he were a real boogeyman.
Which he was. And no one said
a word, he was that wealthy."

"What did he do with the kids?"

"Ate them. God knows. In the end
whatever he did, they died.
All his wealth couldn't provide
enough pleasure but allowed
him to pursue these dark things,
and in the midst of all this
he spent all his money.
So to try to keep living
his accustomed life he sought

out the Philosopher's Stone,
just to make some gold.
And to do so he sent word
across Europe that he would
need an alchemist, and found
Prelati, from Italy,
who quickly set up a lab.
But Prelati's personal
beliefs about alchemy
included asking Satan
directly for what they sought,
and locals began finding
magic circles in the woods
where Prelati and Laval
had tried to summon Satan.
And kids kept going missing.
Almost every night they went
out into the dark forest,
drew an enormous circle
with a horrible powder
made of sulfur and dried blood,
probably from the children,

and in that circle they drew
a pentagram, and invoked
the devil, calling on him
to rise up from the center.
And, they believed, with their spells
they could bind him and compel
him to give them their desire,
which shows you their arrogance,
that a supernatural beast,
who had the power to test
Jesus himself, remember,
could be called forth like a servant
and bossed around. But Satan
played hard to get and Laval
and Prelati tried harder
to convince him they were both
worthy of him. Prelati
eventually proposed
sacrificing the liver,
heart, lungs, and eyes of a child.
So the Maréchal de Rais
was like, 'Absolutely man,

I do that shit all the time.'
So they did that, more of that,
until finally young boys
and girls were disappearing
so frequently that protests
erupted in town and marched
to his castle gates. The Church
was compelled to get involved.
A bishop personally
pressured a duke to arrest
Laval and Prelati both,
and charge them with sorcery
and murder and sodomy.
And in the trial, everything
came out. Prelati ratted
on Laval and told how he
took insane pleasure stabbing
the children after using them
and then closely observed
the quivering of their flesh
the rhythmic spurting of blood
the light fading from their eyes.

He confirmed a hundred kids
from surrounding villages
had been taken in three years.
But the Maréchal de Rais
was so haughty he refused
to even speak in the court.
They were condemned to be burned
alive, but even in death
the wealthy are better off—
they strangled the Maréchal
before they threw his body
on the pyre, while Prelati
burned alive. The ashes
of Laval were gathered up
and left for his family.
Prelati's ashes were thrown
into the wind and scattered."

"That's definitely a rough day.
It kind of puts mine
in perspective. No one died,
or was eaten, and Satan

didn't rise up from the ground.
Unless that was Satan's pinch
on my ass, putting his mark
on me. It wouldn't surprise
me to find a pentagram
on the floor of her office."

"The thing about Laval though,
it's not funny. At all."

"Oh no. It's just terrible."

"We can joke about Satan
or the boogeyman, but this
was real. I mean, it is real,
it happened. One hundred kids.
Imagine what their parents
went through, knowing that monster
lived among them. Imagine
the children, how terrified
they must have been when they knew
what was going to happen.

Oh my god, it's so awful,"
and she rolled over. I hugged
her and brushed the hair from her
forehead. Maybe the next book
she worked on would be about
grifters and their many tricks,
something light. I felt her fall
asleep under my fingers.
But I wasn't sleepy yet.
How could I be? Satanic
Frenchmen were just the latest
distraction—I'd also walked
out on my job, my so-called
wonderful opportunity
to do work that I love,
to work with books, but I walked
out on how stupid it was.
And I walked out on my boss.
And I had no idea
what I would do tomorrow.
And partly to put tomorrow off
and partly because my mind

was racing, I thought to read
a book, though my head was stuffed
with stories, so I picked up
THEY ALL SEEMED ASLEEP, which was
lying beside the bed,
remembering I'd meant to
read it when it was published
last year and everyone had
something to say about it,
though I forget what that was.
My former professor Ken
said he'd liked it; it was short.

                    The ping, the ping of shroud lines
                    in mooring slips in the dark
                    laughter and hawsers creaking
                    something warm, a breeze inside
                    the breeze, surrounded our ship
                    and pulled us into the dock
                    Molly stepped out of the fog
                    and threw us the line   distant

thunder seemed like fake thunder
we pulled against her and she
pulled us in   the downtown lights
quivered like a plant in mist
and I stepped ashore   the boat
and I weren't friends and the crew
was like my public high school
I ignored their shouts and walked
straight ahead over the damp
cobblestones and broken glass
to Molly holding the line
she wouldn't look at me, she
fastened the boat to the pier
fine, I thought, I'll spend my gold
on wine   the air was busy
with the fluttering of bats
and roasted meat   a light rain
fell sideways or hung in the
air   my clothes were out of date
I walked in the direction
of the streetlights and came to
a bar and went in and said

"I have seen a great ship pulled
down by bickering
and mismanagement. Give me a drink"
the silence
that greeted me wore angry
black helmets and carried guns
and these big men looked at me
with empty eyes   I went back out
the whole city was armed
and now I noticed shouting
in a square off to the right
in torchlight, so I headed
up the street and joined the crowd
they cheered as a man was raised
awkward, impaled on a pole

which swayed as they tried to hold
it up, so his arms were flung
like a puppet's, and shadows
made his face seem to flicker
everyone around me cheered
and spilled their drinks   I backed out

of the square and stood frozen
in the changing shadows and
light   then I started to walk
backwards at first then hurried
to the ship at the harbor
some of the crew stood around
with Molly in their arms   Molly
like a flask of shipboard rum
"What the hell is going on
in this town?" but she didn't
answer   laughter   the harbor
licked the bottoms of the boats
one of the crew came towards me
and said "what's your problem, man?"
the others set Molly down
I walked back up the stone street
with no ideas   nowhere
I still hadn't had a drink
and that was next on my list
perpetually   also
a much easier job
I walked back into town

to the central square, to wait
for a bus   one was idling
without a driver   I got on it
sat in the back
leaned against the window
watched the citizens move
through the streets in groups as if
something glorious happened
the gentle idling put me
to sleep and when I woke up
we were climbing the hills
out of town   much too dark to see
who was accompanying me
this night   they all seemed asleep
for a while the stark shadows
held me   only my mind moved
wildly behind my eyes
until I heard a tiny
song coming from the driver
song of a bandit's broken
heart, song of his betrayal
I slept and dreamed I was awake

until the hilltops lightened
the bus leveled out and we
rolled in neutral silently
into the high-valley
desert-town
anonymity
that simply comes to a stop
beyond the farthest houses
suspicious dogs raised their heads
birds on aerials lifted off
a little smoke from a fire
wind, coffee percolating
in a shop
the opposite
of a harbor town   almost
disappearing in the sky
the bus stopped before a church
none of the passengers went in
I followed a girl
in a long rustic cape
to a dark shop   smell of bread
flies bouncing on the window

coffee, sugar-dusted roll
two coins in a stoneware jar
I sat in a sunny doorway
what would be my next move?
it was the summer solstice
I always thought of that day
as beginning summer's end
melancholy bright sunlight
and the bravado of June
dusted off my pants and walked
around, wished I had a book
wondered why I left my bag
on the ship   I must have meant it
a sub-rosa challenge
to the part of me in charge
now no clothes or books, just gold
coins, scrap of paper
on the paper was written:
"stars spearfishing in the sea
costa del sol, second watch"
it seemed more important then
I walked to a park and sat

for a while then took a nap
circular leaves of poplars
fanned the breeze all around me
woke up slowly to a crow
approaching with mischief
back down the road to a bar
open for lunch   a woman
wearing a white hat nodded
all I could see was white
in the dark   three voices fell
and the darkness was complete
I took a seat at the bar
and ordered a beer   the drink
I forgot to drink in port
beautiful dim-lit liquor
I'd have to go buy some clothes
and sleep somewhere   "Can I sleep
here?" She looked at me blankly
"Do you have rooms or just beer?"
"We have liquor too, and snacks"
one of the three voices sat
next to me   his sister had room

"another round please"
he said, "you came on the bus?"
"Is there any other way?"
He smiled then   "What brings you here?"
"I quit my job, I hopped on
the bus, that's about how far
I thought it out" He ordered
more drinks and invited me
to his sister's place that night
for dinner   "What are your plans
till then?" he asked, "because
I'm going to smoke this at the lake"
a small, badly twisted joint
the lake was the same color
as the sky and full of clouds
it was humming, getting loud
I didn't want to panic
a heavy weight on the back
of my neck   I slumped lower
in the dry sedge   I didn't know
the guy's name   "uh, hey man
what's your name and what's that sound?"

A slow grin rose
from his teeth and he pointed
up   a jet humming
six miles over our heads   "Jim"
he said   "Thank you Jim, now I'm
too high to meet your sister"
he laughed   three wild ducks flew up
"You'll have a lot in common"
the ducks settled on the lake
I knew nothing about Jim
or this town, my coming here
was accidental, my job
was back in port where the town
was gripped by some madness
no matter who that was, stuck
over their heads in the square
even if he did something
miraculously evil
even a despotic madman
torturer, breaker of minds
everything became clear then

by the lake   clear   I shivered
Jim stood up and packed a pack
of cigarettes   sound returned
which I hadn't heard   he held
out his hand and pulled me up
light broke apart on the lake
the road back, blue stones set in
other stones, the sky dropping
all around Jim, sky of smoke
around him   at the town's edge
an old woman approaching
bow-legged, incredibly
dark in a black bikini
when she passed us Jim said "She
always wears that, she's going
down to the lake"
many ideas fled me
but none of them through language
and then Jim stopped, knocking on
a weathered wood door   "Get off
your ass"   he yelled   "company,
paying company"   he smiled

"don't worry, it's cheap"   I smiled
but didn't mean it, I felt
like a little boy being
led around by an older
possibly malevolent
boy in the schoolyard   the door
opened and his sister was
plain   that was a big relief
smell of fish fried long ago
dim light, thick green carpeting
my new temporary home
dinner was a casserole
on the couch in the blue light
of an enormous TV
and when the feeling left me
through my knees
my confidence returning
I asked them what they had heard
about the port town, violence
lawlessness, executions
they hadn't heard anything
"Nothing in the newspaper?"

"No one reads the newspaper"
"What I saw there was crazy
they, they, just executed
a man and laughed"
"Oh here's where she throws her drink
right in the director's face!"
the sister said and Jim laughed
evidently he knew this story
a show on celebrities
a martini to the face
and more laughter from TV   I tried
asking them again   anything about it
any political news
Jim and his sister just shook
their heads like they were warding
off flies and turned their burnt gazes
to a small saucer of drugs—
their news briefing over, the
evening turned frivolous
and I was shown to my bed
in the extra room beside
the garage and there I dreamed

my dreams and forgot each one
morning came through the dusty
curtains   the day stretched ahead
of me empty, completely
unformed, mare's tails in the sky
I lay there for a long time
bacon and eggs and the old smell
of fish filled me with unease
and I couldn't remember
her name   she stood in a cloud
of cigarette smoke and grease
"You sleep ok?"   "A little
stationary"   "uh, what
do you mean?"   "My last job was on
a ship"   "You were a sailor?"
"Well I wouldn't say sailor—
I worked on a ship is all
never mind   breakfast smells good"
"You got any plans today?"
she asked   "I was thinking
of checking out the town, you know
I haven't had a day off

in a long time, what would you
do?"   "Me? I'd take the bus back
to the port, there's nothing here"
"Why don't you leave then?"   "Me, leave?"
she gave me a plate of eggs
she didn't look like she'd leave
she sat down at the counter
we drank coffee in silence
the days all started like this
for a month   I walked around
and ended up in the bar
the idea is not to think
about your life passing
and it seems not to   the bar
was small and quiet, no one
talked to me unless Jim came
and he had little to say
there were comfortable seats
cold beer and country music
timeless, dim, anonymous
until Don bought me a drink
he knew I'd come from the port

and what was going on there
"what IS going on there, Don?"
he looked at me pointedly
"What did you see there?" he asked

"It was crazy   I've been there
several times   it used to be
a regular port   hookers
bars, drugs, thriving black market
but normal   essentially
peaceful   the police had it
under control   this time
it was crazy   I saw a man . . ."
I winced instead of finish
"You saw them impale Stewart"
"Who's Stewart?" I asked "and why
I mean, what the fuck happened?"
"The nationalist party
seized power there in a coup
bloodless   for a few minutes
the opposition was weak
they rolled over and hoped

for the best   most of the people
support the new leader"
"Who is . . . ?"   "His name is The Cat"
"What happened?"
"The opposition was in power
and their progressive
legislation was too much
for, you know, the usual
characters   priests, big fat cops
old ladies, busybodies
they passed a law making it
legal for gay people
to own businesses   first the Church
was up in arms—for real—guns
were blessed at special masses
and some people died   The Cat
is a colonel and he led
the coup   but where have you been?"
"I was at sea"   we both drank
"It's fucking barbarism"
I said after a long while
he looked at me closely then

and nodded slowly   "Are you...?"
I asked, and he said "Yes, and you?"
"Not me" I said, "but fuck them
why doesn't anybody
stand up to fascist bullies?
My theory is they'd crumple
the minute we inflicted
any pain   they're big babies"
Don said "we?"   "Well" I said, "'we'
meaning rational people
who won't fucking stand for it
and want to see some justice"
Don was leaning back, looking
smug or pleased or something
"do continue"   "no, no, you're right
I'll stop talking, I don't know
anything about all this"
"It sounds like you do" he said
"what do you mean?"   "what do YOU
mean?"   "Don" I said, getting up,
"I have to use the restroom"
when I came back there were more drinks

"On that ship—did you ever
have occasion to work with
ordnance?"   "The cannons, you mean?
I know how the cannons work
I guess, but what I don't know
Don, is what you're getting at"
"Would you like to see a cave?"
"Don, I'm not really sure I want
to see any cave now"
He stood up and said "let's go"
stars glimmered on his dented
car, clear piercing emptiness
breathing in the air at night
a drive into the high hills
two or three lights, a dirt road
"Tell me more about The Cat"
"The Cat was born to be The Cat
cruelty, money, summer light
all conspired to make him
who he is—like a jaguar
on hind legs
quoting Socrates and Poe"

"Quoting Poe?"   "He's well-read,
idiots think that's amazing
despite their scorn   don't be fooled
by idiots, they know they're dumb
that's why they're so dangerous"
"What did he actually do?"
"Some helicopters appeared
over the prime minister's tennis court
at night   he played at night
no one ever saw him
again and The Cat said
some things in Latin, fist raised,
surrounded by priests, and said
'tear this country's cancer out
wherever you see it'
meaning: 'everyone who's mad
about something, or too weak
to admit they might be to blame
for a part of their own
dumb misfortune   and has guns,
run amok, killing any
kind of person who ever

pissed you off or made you feel
insecure—please, go ahead'
and they did, and they're not done
gay people rounded up
newspapers shut down, editors killed
they didn't even pretend
to imprison people first
and they're still doing it too"
parked in utter darkness
vertigo of following
a stranger on a dirt path
no trees this high, just the wind
"So I saw Stewart impaled—
who was he?" "One of our guys"
Don said, stopping and turning
to face me, though I couldn't
see his face "someone sold him
out   someone working for us"
I didn't say anything
"I need to know who that is
maybe you can help"
I shouldn't have had the last

drink I had in the bar
always a depressing thought
the arid mountain stood up
above me and I staggered
beneath it or what Don said
who seemed an awful lot like
a dangerous, paranoid
spy who thinks I'm a spy too
"Don all I did
was see some shit
happen I wish I hadn't
and then got on a night bus
which didn't even charge me
and let me off way up here
and now I'm drunk and walking
to a cave"   it mollified
him or he already knew
a sudden lantern lit up
the cave's mouth and we went in
till then, my thinking on armed
insurrection was shallow
I was for it, in theory

for the result, which had to
be better than what we had
or the inability
at least to imagine something better
seemed brutish, but the armed part
was a real turnoff

after the scene I witnessed
in port   and the inevitable
destruction of the good
the revolution in France
all the blood poured on the vines
loud brutes like Marat shouting
until Reason turns its face
and beautiful women's heads
bob on the ends of tall poles
Sendero Luminoso
too—not a bad idea
in the realm of ideas
that never should be realized
on Earth   but what a great name
Shining Path   I was thinking

when I focused
on my surroundings   the cave
low lit, lanterns on the ground
disappearing down into
the mountain darkness   movement
murmurs   oily clicking guns
the blackness was physical
reaching in from all around
an immense sneering liquid
Don took my elbow and led me
to the farthest reaches
of the light past ten or twelve
people unpacking some crates
and pulled a big blue tarp off
three old French .75s
"Howitzers?" I said, "what for?"
"For shelling the town of course
what else are howitzers for?"
"This town though? what's going on?"
and also, do I want to know this?
should you be telling me this?
It's been a long night

but we just met"   Don put back
the tarp and sat on a rock
"Stewart was a good soldier"
Don said, "though he was really
a bartender in real life
his job was to tail The Cat
so we could find his weakness
he was double-crossed and now
The Cat knows we're here   he'll come
here himself to round us up"
"Not if you can shell him first?"
"Exactly   and we need you
to do the shelling, sailor"
I thought I argued quite well
their superior fire power   helicopters
my personal disinterest in this civil war
Don patiently described
The Cat's horrors, the campaign
against the interesting,
the doubtful, the terrific
in this world, poets digging
their own graves, though half-assed,

festive teens shot in
community theaters, their
parents seeing the whole cast
humiliated in death
even in the best of times
the rich getting out of jail
or never going in
freedom of speech a sham
free-speech zones at demonstrations
citizens of the empire
arrested and held without charges
or put in airplanes
and tortured in aerial
secrecy, above all laws
more of this for an hour
my face in my hands, a deeper
dark   Don got up and returned
with a wisp of a woman
in a short white summer dress
she spoke to me like a mouse
"how do you like   the underworld?"

she was barefoot   she almost
glowed in the cave   much later
I realized what everyone
else knows   the rebellion isn't
as sexy as the rebels
Delphine was her name   Don drove
me back to Jim's sister's house
with a pistol and a map
I didn't want the pistol
but he and Delphine were firm
it was too late to turn back

Jim's sister was staring at
a newspaper at breakfast
and ignoring me   "What's up?"
"My horoscope says I'm fat"
"You're not fat, plus, it doesn't
know you"   "It said I'd meet you"
and she held the paper out
to me   the headlines said
MILITARY CRACKS DOWN
ON TERRORISTS IN HILLS

something occurred in my brain
the idea of loud noise
and sickening dizziness
she looked at me   "Where were you
last night?"   panic   a headband
of panic oozed out of me
"you look terrible   how drunk
were you?"   drunk   what a relief
I settled back   "Really drunk
what does it say about me
in there?"   she showed me
STRANGER WILL PROVIDE MONETARY
ASSISTANCE WHEN YOU NEED IT
my weak smile   I was way out
of my league   I cracked
before breakfast
and now The Cat was coming
for me, I was a headline
excusing myself, arming myself
I went to the bar
closed   it was just 9 a.m.
I had no idea what

Don or Delphine did by day
walked nervously down the street
walked the other way   hurried
past the police station door
hoped I would see one of them
and did accidentally
see Delphine just as the jeeps arrived
stopped in the dust in the square
she was delivering bread
in an old white panel truck
our eyes met, she made a face
and slipped from the truck
into confusing courtyards

soldiers in black uniforms
swarmed the truck
set it alight
it burned awhile then blew up
I was in a shop watching
with some others, then we ran
out the back, through the alleys
I hid by the lake all day

creeping back at night I saw
the old bikini woman
dead on the side of the road
horrible bright umbrella
of lights over the town square
but silence, creepy, just me
walking up the dirt road home
the pistol felt unearthly
heavy, I looked towards the cave
there was nowhere else to go
still dark when I heard the click
of a gun and a loud hiss
"I'm a friend" I said   silence
reached out to me, then my arm
taken by a strong grip
pulled into the cave
where everything was moving
in near darkness   guns cocking
grenades passed from hand to hand
"You know what? I've been thinking"
I said to the dark figures
nearby   "if we shell the town . . ."

Delphine sidled up to me
she smelled like cypress branches
she stood very close
her open palm on my chest
"You'll shell the town when we're gone
then you'll leave   they'll come up here
you know, curiosity
killed The Cat   we'll be waiting"
"Why would The Cat come himself?"
"Because he's The Cat, that's why
he's fearless, he'll be the first"
they shuffled heavily out
surely there is a statue
somewhere to honor the man
they leave behind with the stuff

and promise that they'll return
the new member of the group
a kiss on tiptoes
like being left on the moon
standing in the cave between
darkness and darker darkness

with an army approaching
groping for the howitzers
pulling back the heavy breech
too loud   stupidly cowering
in the dark   more groping
for the .75 shells
without thinking
they'd already been sighted
all I had to do was pull
the halyard and plug my ears
the question of violence
and its utility plagued me
the moment
before a cataclysm
both irreversible
and preventable is calm
and utterly still   reason
appears to fill the air
but an inconsequential
movement, a finger twitching
or a word, rips everything
apart and sets in motion

what can't be put back   a dead
woman, families murdered
with painstaking glee or crushed
by a bomb dropped from the clouds
there should be a horrible
statue of remembrance
where everyone can see it
a huge finger on a trigger
a mysterious birdsong
rippled across the valley
waking me out of these thoughts
I yanked hard on the halyard
and the big gun leapt at me
only later did I hear it
in a few seconds a flash
in the town, then brighter light
flames, wildly swinging search lights

the other two guns hit
military vehicles
water dripped deep in the cave
I climbed and sat high above

the cave behind some rockfall
and waited   nothing happened
for a long time, nothing moved
around me or in the town
I hoped they'd all disappeared
down along the valley's edge
a ribbon of lighter sky
the stillness turning bluer
then from the nearby scrub oak
a single bunting whistled
and was silent   another
bunting farther down whistled
what exactly do they say
to each other?   it all sounds
exactly the same, it sounds
like the call is the answer
or it's a competition
Messiaen transcribed their songs
on his walks, a composer
told me, but we will never
get any closer than that
imitation   chewing my

fingernails I thought about
the composer I had known at home
a warmth came up through the breeze
it was unaccountably
shivery   then I noticed
low susurrations, engines
at the base of the mountain
pulled from reverie
and shocked to see a platoon
ranged up and down
the slope   I cowered, then peeked
throughout the coming assault
I listened but couldn't hear
Delphine or Don, their people
were supposed to be nearby
but the soldiers fanned out
their approach, and the terrain
was so open and treeless
where would they heroically
erupt from to liberate
me and also the country?
a terrible heaviness

pressed me to the dust   the sun
was up now, halfway over
the ridge, I heard loose rocks
trembling down the mountainside
soldiers whispering
a bunting whistled nearby
more insistently this time
then dozens more down the slope
answered, and then the scrub oak
some of it   raised from the ground
where it was affixed to hats
and opened up with small arms
the noise pummeled me, the air
seemed to pound me to the dirt
and I missed what happened next
but saw the results   soldiers lay
in terrible poses
and Don's people were firing
into the cave where The Cat
had been forced by the attack
I raised myself up to see
Delphine thirty yards below

holding what looked like a phone
and talking   the reply
was a huge shock up my legs
that sat me down and a roar
as the cave exploded out
the mountainside, flinging rocks
and dust like a huge hose
into the valley, killing
Don and Delphine and six more
of their people   it seems they
miscalculated the charge
or something, they had no idea
what they were really doing
though their trap was impressive
really impressive   I rose
to my knees, I was shaky

high ringing tones in my ears
full sunlight filtering through
the hanging plume of dust
The Cat was dead, soldiers all
dead, Don and Delphine were dead
wearing scrub-oak hats   soon I heard

weeping and footsteps   I climbed
down and found three of the gay
revolutionaries crying
in the broken rocks all down
on their knees pulling their hair
for these the blasted bodies
of their comrades   I went down
to them and stood beside them
and looked with them at their friends
and after a time I walked
over to two dead soldiers
every one with broken teeth
and still dribbling blood, bones
horribly white in the daylight

less than a minute ago
they were all alive, swearing
under their breath, distracted by love
or hate   now they all seemed asleep

The sound of wind blowing rain
against the windows brought me
back from the arid mountains

to the bedroom, the warm bed,
my wife breathing long and deep
beside me. I switched the light
off and listened to the rain.
The night was another story
happening outside, stretching
outwards, maybe forever.
And from her rapid twitching
eyes I knew my wife contained
another story this night,
a dream that once or twice curled
her lip for her while she slept.
I kissed her forehead. She moaned.
And then I too drifted off
rather precipitously
into a dark, windy place
familiar to me, the dream.

        And in the dream I am back
        in Ann Arbor, in the rich
        orange light of mid-1970s
        summer evening, no parents
        at all, they are blocks away.

Gliding around cul-de-sacs
on my dream bike with dream friends
I never actually
see, I just have the feeling
of them peripherally.
Landscape of duplex condos
made of dark wood with sharp roofs.
On the fringe where my street turns
but the trees continue, woods
stretching away towards Dearborn
or some equally unknown
place, stands a retaining wall
of railroad ties, dark, oily
stacked on top of each other.
Sticking out of one of them
is a very large deer knife,
a low humming comes from it,
I have the sense with my friends
who remain invisible
that it still quivers, just stuck
there by the boogeyman,
and then too much background noise,
a sinister orchestra

just before curtains rise,
and a kid I don't know comes up
looking scared and excited
about the enormous knife.
He tells me who left it there.
Black Leather. That's the guy's name.
And though I've never heard it
before, in that dreamy way
I suddenly understand
all of Black Leather's horrors.
I know. In the dream I've known
it always, and Black Leather
is a fearsome rambling man
moving always in shadow,
passing through the trees at night.
I'm electrified with fear,
and when I look down
the knife is gone. The humming
hasn't stopped though. All my friends
are frantic, like scared chickens:
Black Leather's here! He could be
looking at us from the trees.

The light of the dream changes
to match the new mood. The wind
blows papers and leaves around.
A strange compulsion moves me
towards the line of trees to see
what the other kids can see.
Deep in the woods they're pointing:
Do you see? Can you see it?
I can see nothing.
Everyone's crowded against
the dark wall of railroad ties
separating our housing
development from darkness,
vines, spirits of the forest.
Do you see? Can you see it?
Deep in the trees, way back there,
actually hidden from view,
but understood, and then seen
in my mind, are small railroad tracks.
Black Leather's railroad tracks.
For he appears to use them
to travel the woods at night

on a tiny, evil train
and that I cannot see
this but my friends can
terrifies me. What else
passes so close to my house
every night, what phantom road
traveled by cackling faeries
moving beneath my window?
I stare hard into the gloom
while the horror sounds of dreams
rise around me like a train
in my ears. Was this the train
they were trying to show me?
If I could just see the
miniature railroad tracks
the horrible sound would stop,
but when I turn to my friends
they remain just out of sight.
I can hear them and sense them
and grow more frantic, turning
wildly around, calling out,
hearing nothing but laughter,

laughter coming from a spot
inside my own head. And what
does that mean? Who is doing
all this laughing? Who told me
about Black Leather? I think
finally he is something
I have been telling myself,
and this thought tears me right out
of the dream.

I lie in bed.

My wife asleep next to me.

Two people in a little room

in an enormous city

dreaming
after a hard day

the same as all the others.

Acknowledgments

THEY ALL SEEMED ASLEEP first appeared
as a chapbook from Octopus Books, 2008.

Thank you to my readers—Joshua Beckman,
Heidi Broadhead, David Caligiuri, Srikanth
Reddy, and Matthew Zapruder. Your assistance
and encouragement are beyond measure.